ANNA DEAVERE SMITH

House Arrest and Piano

Anna Deavere Smith is an actor, a teacher, a playwright, and the creator of an acclaimed series of one-woman plays based on her interviews with diverse voices from communities in crisis. She has won two Obie Awards, two Tony nominations for her play *Twilight: Los Angeles, 1992*, and a MacArthur Fellowship, and she was a Pulitzer Prize finalist for her play *Fires in the Mirror*. She has had roles in the films *Philadelphia*, *An American President*, and *The Human Stain*, and she has worked in television on *The Practice*, *Presidio Med*, and *The West Wing*. She is the founder and director of the Institute on the Arts and Civic Dialogue and is a University Professor at New York University, with an appointment in the Tisch School of the Arts and an affiliation with the School of Law.

House Arrest

and

Piano

ANNA DEAVERE SMITH

TWO PLAYS

House Arrest
A Search for American Character In and Around the White House, Past and Present

and

Piano

ANCHOR BOOKS

A DIVISION OF RANDOM HOUSE, INC. • NEW YORK

AN ANCHOR BOOKS ORIGINAL, FEBRUARY 2004

Library of Congress Cataloging-in-Publication Data
Smith, Anna Deavere.
House arrest : a search for American character in and around the White House, past and present ; and Piano : two plays / Anna Deavere Smith.
p. cm.
"An Anchor Books original"—T.p. verso.
ISBN 1-4000-3357-8
1. Political plays, American. 2. Historical drama, American. 3. White House (Washington, D.C.)—Drama. 4. United States—Politics and government—Drama. 5. National characteristics, American—Drama. 6. Mass media—Political aspects—Drama. 7. Presidents—Drama. 8. Cuba—Drama. I. Smith, Anna Deavere. Piano. II. Title: Piano. III. Title.
PS3569.M465H68 2004
812'.54—dc22   2003057800

Book design by Debbie Glasserman

www.anchorbooks.com

This volume stands in memory of my mother, Anna Young Smith.

It is dedicated to Congressman Amory and Mrs. Priscilla Houghton.

And in memory of the actresses Gloria Foster and Madge Sinclair, who performed the role of Susanna in *Piano* in different stages of its development and contributed to my idea of this character through their elegance, candor, sophistication, life experience, discipline, presence, strength, femininity, dignity, rigorous critique, and meticulous professionalism.

And to the following actors who performed *House Arrest* in an earlier version at the Mark Taper Forum in Los Angeles in the spring of 1999:

Regina Carter (performer, composer, and violinist)
Chad L. Coleman
Lynette Du Pre
Glenn Fleshler
Crispin Freeman
Francesca Harper
Ezra Knight
Linda Marie Larson
Kimber Riddle
Michele Shay
Eric Steinberg
Bahni Turpin

And to Gordon Davidson.

And to David Chalian, who took care of the five hundred interviews upon which *House Arrest* is based and constantly informed the project with his limitless appetite for American history and current American presidential politics.

And to Stephen Rivers, who helped me navigate Washington, D.C., while writing *House Arrest*.

And to Tania Leon, composer/conductor, who inspired *Piano* through a story she told me about her grandmother.

Special thanks to Douglas Wager, Riley Temple, Stephen Richard, and the Board of Trustees of the Arena Stage Theater, Washington, D.C., 1995–1997, for their support of the development process for *House Arrest*.

Contents

ACT TWO

I. A Scream

II. Sending the Canaries into the Mines

III. Darkness at Noon

IV. *Political Theater*

V. *Moral Slippage*

VI. *One Card at a Time*

PIANO 149

Introduction

House Arrest and *Piano* are set during two periods of American history, a century apart. *Piano* finds its home in a big white mansion on a Cuban sugar plantation at the end of the nineteenth century. *House Arrest* prances and romps through stages of American history, but finds its destination and its starting point in the American White House in Washington, D.C., during the final presidency of the twentieth century. Both plays have characters that represent the media. Both plays question the power of the media in shaping our "truths." Each play has within it a question about history—a question about the authorship of history and the ownership of history. Authorship of history equals power.

If those who have power own the news, create our fantasies, and ultimately own history (as in their word becomes *the* word, unchallenged), the promise of democracy can become frail. This challenge and the consequences of that challenge are best captured in a very passionate moment in a recording of a conversation between the African American author James Baldwin and the white anthropologist Margaret Mead. It was called "A Rap on Race" and was recorded both as a vocal recording on an eight-record set and as a book. The conversation took place in the early seventies. This recording was on sale shortly thereafter in the bookstore of the Museum of Natural History. It was fitting that it should dwell in the same house as stuffed replicas of other species. It was a linguistic exhibition in its own kind of glass case: a recording of the passionate voices of two people battling out the relationships of cultural identities to survival of the human race. Why is the survival of humankind so wrapped up with identity? Why is the survival of humankind so wrapped up with belief systems? The animals know what they know through

DNA. We know what we need to survive through culture and we transmit it through language—and not always so effectively. Why are we so tied to our histories? Why do we fight over our histories, on the one hand, and deny their presence on the other? It is a struggle that threatens to wipe off all life on the planet. Perhaps the threat is more dramatic as we set off on the road of the twenty-first century. And yet it was very dramatic between Mead and Baldwin in the early seventies:*

MEAD:
It is crucial
At the present moment
In history
What the Western world does is crucial.

BALDWIN:
You say history, I say time.

MEAD:
All right
Present time
I am very willing to say either one.
…

BALDWIN:
But you really must consider seriously I think the state of a
       nation in which
I Jimmy
Or I historically
Am forced to say
I do not care what the pursuant facts are
I cannot afford to care.

*Adapted from *A Rap on Race* © 1971 by James Baldwin and Margaret Mead. Copyright renewed.

MEAD:
But you see the significant sentence is "I cannot afford to care."

BALDWIN:
I don't.

MEAD:
That's what I've been talking about all along!
That maybe you can't afford to care/ now/ and I can,
Now what is the difference between the people who cannot
    afford to care about the facts and those who can?
And that's a real difference . . .

BALDWIN:
The difference is that
You generically historically *write* the facts which
I
Am expected to believe.
The difference is that you
Historically,
Generically,
Have betrayed me so often
And lied to me *so long*
That no
Number of facts
According to you
Would ever convince me!

MEAD:
And if that's so/ the world is doomed!
Because if we can't reach a point
Where everybody in this world can understand facts
. . .
You say the truth will never matter to you anymore.

BALDWIN:
I didn't say truth I said facts!

MEAD:
Well facts.
It seems to me that the key sentence here is "I cannot —*afford*—
    to—care—about—the facts."

I worry about those who cannot afford to care about the
"facts." I worry that their educations have not engaged them with
anything beyond the "facts," as if the "facts" were only to be
repeated. Indeed, our educations should lead us to facts and the
questions that arise when the facts have been exhausted. Let's
exhaust the facts, imagine a future, and work to make it real! As
the scholar Cornel West said in an earlier play of mine, *Twilight:
Los Angeles, 1992*, to hope is "to go beyond the evidence to make
new possibilities based on visions that become contagious to
allow us to engage in heroic actions always against the odds." This
idea potentially distinguishes the work of the artist from the work
of the historian. It could also lead the artist, the historian, and the
activist to new collaborations.

In writing historical plays, I am writing a reaction *to*, rather
than a record *of*, history. I see actors as important embodiments
of that reaction to history. Actors are the artists who deal with
"presence" as a phenomenon. Presence is the tool of the actor
just as paint and brushes are the tools of the painter.

More than any other theater practitioner, it is the actor's task
to make history present. Actors can make the future present.
They can make the unreal present. It is in their presence that we
can react to history. Unlike in the courtroom, where a forced
truth is required to end the display of murky truths, theater
embraces the murky truth as tragic, as absurd, and if we are
lucky, as inspiring. When the actor makes the future present for
us, we can react to the possibility of a future. When we are con-

fronted with both the past and the future, we may become ener-
gized to reimagine and adjust our present.

To me, plays are potential catalysts for social change. History
seems to belong to those who survive and those who can record
it. For writers who have access to being published, the claim is
obvious. But there are also those who claim history in poems, in
music, in hip-hop, in rap, in folk songs, in hymns, in holy books,
in graffiti, in a print, in dances.

History also belongs to those who *could* afford to care about
the facts, those who fought for the facts, fought for a correction
of the facts. This puts the writing of history, the creation of art,
and the recording of memory in a significant light.

Historical plays, as *reorganizations* of history—interactions
with history, reactions *to* history, metaphors *for* history—become
more and more potentially useful in such a complicated world
as ours in the year 2003, the world we now refer to as the "Post
September 11 world." It is *crucial* (to use that word with the same
intensity as Margaret Mead delivers it) that the facts matter to
us—as the beginning of a conversation. I understand what Baldwin suggests, that people do decide *not* to care about the facts.

Perhaps the facts are hard to find, as *House Arrest* would suggest. In the word war that goes on in politics and the word circus
ring-mastered by the media, one begins to question if there *are*
any real facts. And if there are, what's their relevance? Those
who want ideological and electoral power grab hold of the
"facts" and "spin" them. It's dizzying. This ultimately affects the
way we engage with our educations and with our civic lives. It
threatens to disempower us in the face of the amount of vigi-
lance it takes to keep the pleasures of democracy alive. It affects
how we see ourselves as citizens in the world at large and, ultimately, how we engage with the fate of all of human life.

These plays, these reorganizations of history, are also meant
to try to bring another type of very practical truth to the American theater. For many years I have been in a quandary about

why so many of those who strut across the stages of such a multicultural society as ours . . . are white. The nontraditional casting movement of the eighties was similarly puzzled. It tried to find a way to make theater more democratic, by suggesting that we all could play anything. Some considered it an ill-fated version of affirmative action. It never got wings. In the theater, in the arts in general, there is no Supreme Court. Decisions are subjective and have to do with desire and dreams, which are mysterious. Those mysteries cannot and should not be legislated. In fact, the courts are not the most imaginative way to face social challenges. We see the limits of the law. We look to art to fill the spiritual gap. The theater, movies, and television have not made as much headway as the world would suggest is needed.

An actor is a metaphor, a walking, breathing metaphor. An actor is a person whose identity is for rent—not for sale, but for rent. He/she is someone who pursues the other. And in a world where the lines are being more harshly drawn every moment, I feel the yet unfulfilled promise of the actor.

Even as the actor has the potential to be the other, *all others*, the tension between the self and other is real. In *House Arrest*, actors should play across gender and race. Yet, this does not mean that their evident race and gender is nonexistent or insignificant. The contrary is the case. Their evident race and gender is on one side of the bridge, and the other they pursue is across the bridge. The effort to cross that bridge is the drama, and it should not be denied.

In writing *Piano*, I was specifically looking for a time and place in American history in which people of all different races could be in one living room. Hence Cuba, at the turn of the century. Africans, Spaniards, Indians, and Asians found their way, and ultimately they mixed their races. In this play, the evident race and culture that the actor represents onstage is important. It is also exciting to work in such a multicultural community as the one that *Piano* requires. In this play we also see the turning of a servant class into a powerful class. We see those who are the subjects strive to become the authors of their history.

These two plays react to history and are dedicated to encouraging those who produce, direct, design, market, and perform them to get closer and closer to caring passionately about what the facts are, caring passionately about what the truth is and was. They invite research and passionate debate during the creative process. Ultimately, the goal is to involve the audience in that passion. These two plays, based on facts, take dramatic license and are offered not as truths, but as fictions that attempt to tell other truths, the kinds of truths that live in fiction and in imaginary worlds.

Anna Deavere Smith
New York City
February 2004

House Arrest

A Search for American Character In and Around
the White House, Past and Present

Production Credits

House Arrest was originally commissioned and produced by the Arena Stage, Washington, D.C., on November 7, 1997. Doug Wager, Artistic Director.

It was subsequently produced by the Mark Taper Forum in Los Angeles, Gordon Davidson, Artistic Director. It premiered on April 9, 1999.

Its original New York production was provided by the Public Theater, George C. Wolfe, Producer. It opened at the Public Theater on March 26, 2000.

Special thanks to the Goodman Theatre.

Special thanks to the Intiman Theatre.

General Production Notes

House Arrest is a form of documentary theater. It requires a different kind of acting than psychological realism and depends on an "informed actor."

This play is about real events, using the words of real people. The audience should be made aware of that. Slides should be used, if possible, to announce each character and to inform the audience that the words in the play are verbatim from interviews. A slide with the following language should begin the show, just after lights down, and before any other visual image:

"All words spoken by speakers in the twentieth century are verbatim from interviews conducted by Anna Deavere Smith, unless otherwise noted. All other materials are verbatim from historic texts."

The audience also needs to be given a background on the events. This can be achieved by the use of dramaturgical notes, but it can also be included in the body of the play—with visual aids such as slides and videos, if possible. The overall context of the play is the Clinton administration and the relationship of President Clinton to the press.

The actor's accuracy of language is important. All of the utterances, every "uh" and other nonverbal sounds, where noted, are rhythmic beats that inform the development of character. Many times a character speaks in a counterintuitive way, in which words in and of themselves do not make sense. The play has been written as an extension of research done by the author on the relationship of language to identity. It is recommended that a specific person be included on the production team who gives line notes and makes corrections. The process of playing the play and speaking the words in their exact presentation is the core of the technique of performing the play.

Music and sound effects are useful and important for flow. In all initial productions, original music was composed.

Costumes, stage sets, and props can be as minimal or as ornate as one imagines. The play is performed in bare feet, except when shoes are meant to make a specific statement. Bare feet signify the idea of walking in someone else's shoes.

The author sees actors as cultural workers, who reach toward that which is "other" than themselves, who reach toward that which is different from themselves. To this extent, typecasting should only be used in relationship to casting that is about that reach for the other. People should be cast across race, age, and gender lines. The play is vocally and verbally demanding and requires first and foremost actors with a good vocal and physical range and a facility with language and movement.

Many pieces start with the note (*In reality*), and there follows a description of the age, race, and gender of the speaker. This is only as a frame of reference. It is not suggested or necessary to cast as such.

Characters

All of the characters are people who are alive or who were alive. They can be played by a company of one or more actors. Actors play several different roles. Gender and race do not need to match those of the characters listed.

STUDS TERKEL

GEORGE STEPHANOPOULOS

CINDER STANTON

PENNY KISER

KEN BURNS

JAMES CALLENDER

ROGER KENNEDY

ANNETTE GORDON-REED

PRESIDENT THOMAS JEFFERSON

EUGENE FOSTER

R. W. APPLE

WALTER TROHAN

LIZZIE MCDUFFIE

BERNARD ASBELL

MICHAEL K. FRISBY

GARY HART

PEGGY NOONAN

ELIZABETH KECKLEY

PRESIDENT ABRAHAM LINCOLN

BRIAN PALMER

WALT WHITMAN

BEN BRADLEE

GLORIA STEINEM

GOVERNOR ANN RICHARDS

ALICE WATERS

GRAYDON CARTER

ANONYMOUS MAN

JUDITH BUTLER

ANITA HILL

MAGGIE WILLIAMS

ALEXIS HERMAN

ED BRADLEY

CHRISTOPHER HITCHENS

WALTER SHAPIRO

DAVID KENDALL

MIKE ISIKOFF

CHRIS VLASTO

PRESIDENT WILLIAM JEFFERSON CLINTON

PRESIDENT GEORGE HERBERT BUSH

FLIP BENHAM

CHERYL MILLS

PAULETTE JENKINS

BLESE CANTY

As the lights go down:

Slide: All words spoken by speakers in the twentieth century are verbatim from interviews conducted by Anna Deavere Smith, unless otherwise noted. All other materials are verbatim from historic texts.

Slide: Act One

Slide: I. Frame

Slide: Studs Terkel, Americanist Radio Host

"Clowns"

(In reality STUDS TERKEL *is a white man in his nineties.)*

(Wearing a trench coat, red socks, Hush Puppies, carrying a cane, and wearing small fedora hat.)

Ya know, when it gets back to as far as guys,
Presidents with dames—
My God!
Ya know!
Kennedy, my God!
It wasn't so much Addison's disease,
he suffered from satyriasis probably!
In fact he said it!
So what?
And my favorite President,
the one
the one President of the century,
major league,
FDR of course,
well FDR is said to have had a fling with a socialite!
And he had polio!
I said my God the man has polio,
this might be very good therapy!
Long before McCarthy there was New Salem.

I think Hillary has a point—
about it being a right-wing. . . .
(But.)
that's too simple!
Well of course they're out to get him!
That's not what the issue is to me!
The issue is—
What the hell have we learned?
Where are we?
I was born in 1912,
the year the *Titanic*,
sank—
the greatest ship ever built—
It hits the tip of an iceberg and bam! It went down.
It went down,
and I came up.
Wow some century!
ANNA DEAVERE SMITH V.O.: What's the defining moment in
    American history?
STUDS TERKEL: Defining moment in American history?
I don't think there's one
you can't say Hiroshima.
That's a big moment.
I don't think there's any one.
I can't pick out any one.
It's a combination of many.
I can't think of any one moment I'd say is the defining moment.
But the gradual slippage—
slippage is the word used by people in
Watergate—
moral slippage.
It's a gradual kind of thing.
A combination of things.
But it's not this—

This almost becomes not the crowning touch,
but the clowning touch!
It's the clowning touch!
It ends with a fright wig,
putty nose,
with baggy pants!
And this is it!
It's not just Clinton and Monica!
We all are wearing the fright wig and putty nose and baggy
    pants!
We're all demeaned!
By that, I mean,
all of us are *clowns* and that's what it's all about!
Instead of a new century
with all the discoveries made,
in medicine—
perhaps more to come
and yet with fewer and fewer people controlling,
more and more and more,
and the more and more and more feeling more and more and
    more
helpless.
And who *runs* the means of communication that condition
    these
people to vote as they vote and think as they think?
We got Lewinsky-ism and Monica-ism!
Instead of "What the hell have we been doing to all these coun-
    tries and
to the have-nots in this country?"
So we're wearing baggy pants, putty nose, and
fright wigs.
We've been *conditioned* to wear them
by this time.
(*Pause.*)

We've—got—to—question—official—truth!
The thing that was so great about Mark Twain!
We honor Mark Twain ya know—
but we don't *read* 'im!
We may read *Huck Finn*—
Even Huck of course was tremendous.
Remember what Huck did?
That great scene on the raft you know—
when Huck
see—
You have to
question official truth!
So truth is the *law* was
A black man is *property* is a *thing*!
And he's *(Huck is)* on with a property named Jim,
a slave, see—
on the raft—
and he heard that Jim says he's going to do a terrible *thing*.
And Huck is thirteen, twelve
and Jim said he's going to look for his wife and kids
and he's gonna *steal* them
from the woman
or person who *owns* them
and Huck says "That woman never did me any harm!
(Whispering.)
I'm—
he's gonna *steal*!
In, in Huck's own mind—
Huck Finn is what it's all about—
the goodness of Huck, you see—
He's an illiterate kid right?
He's had no schoolin'—
But there's something in 'im. *(Whispering, expressive, urgent.)*

And he says "Oh it's a terrible thing, wow what an awful thing
    he's gonna *steal*."
And just then
two slavers caught up!
The guys chasing the slaves —
lookin' for Jim
ya know
and they come up "Anybody on that raft with ya?"
(Pause.)
And Huck yeah (dibdebi)
(They know there's somebody there.)
(Pause.)
"Is he white or black?"
And Huck says
(Pause.)
"*White*."
And they go off.
"Oh my God my conscience"
"I lied!"
Ya know
I lied
and he's gonna —
But if
"I did a terrible thing
(Pause.)
why do I feel so *good*?"
There ya got it!
In Huck
ya captured the human species.
That stuff that Huck is there
that part's been buried!

Slide: Seeing and Being Seen

Slide: George Stephanopoulos, Former Assistant to President Clinton

"The Deal"

(*An attractive, charismatic, white male in his thirties with a fast metabolism.*)

(*Sipping a martini.*)

We're a celebrity culture,
and the President is the Celebrity in Chief.
I think the only private time a President has,
is when he's in the Oval —
and he walks from the Oval
to either his private study or his private bathroom.
That's it!
Once he's in the residence he can move *between* rooms.
But there's still some servants around.
As far as officially, the only truly private time he has is within that
small suite, which is one —
(*He counts.*)
It's four rooms, plus a terrace and one of those rooms is a bath-
     room.
He's sitting at a desk with one of the best views in Washington —
certainly the best morning light I've ever seen in my life —
But it's got glass this thick,
that can't be . . .
touched.
You've got a —

two secretaries on the outside
and two Secret Service people between *them*—
As you move *across* the hall *in* the Oval
there's another room to where,
there's a tiny little pantry and there's another Secret Service
    agent
there—
And then you get to *my* office
And—every—door—
is wired!
Like if I
moved in the back door,
between my office and the Oval
the Secret Service would know! Because it was wired!
And—
I've never thought of it this way before—
What happens, when you juxtapose incredible, immense,
    power?
But the price—
I mean it's a different
um,
it's a different devil's choice!
The price is,
Transparency.
Everything you do is known.
You can be the most *powerful* person in the world *(upward
    inflection)*
you're going to uh,
have every privilege known to man!
Every *whim* is going to be catered to!
The deal is—
You can do whatever you want.
The price is that everybody is going to know
everything you do.

Slide: A Visit to Jefferson's Home at Monticello

Slide: Cinder Stanton, Historian at Monticello

"Pantops"

(CINDER *is center stage on a stool.*)

(*In reality an Anglo-Saxon white woman in her late forties, friendly, down-to-earth, intellectual.*)

Uh.
So
I'm reading something this morning talking about Jefferson
as a landscape designer
and he uses the word *"panoptic"* uh
which means
all-seeing uh.
It can also mean
all *seen* from everywhere
which is interesting.
It's one of those Greek words that uh,
because
Jefferson had named one of his farms
"Pantops" you know based on that,
which means
either seen from everywhere,
or you can see everything *from* there.
Um,
so the whole choice,
of Monticello as a panoptic,

uh *perch*,
basically,
is very very,
Jeffersonian.
(*Pause.*)
He certainly took measures so that he couldn't *be* seen.
But
he bought everything he could see,
and then a hundred yards beyond the line of sight.
So it was obvious,
he was just sort of buying his own
view,
there.
It's interesting, just in relation to what you said in terms of
     modern
Presidents.
That that word has a double meaning.
That they are all-seeing,
or being seen by everyone.

"Justice Is in One Scale"

(In reality a white woman in her late thirties, Southern accent.)

Okay. Okay, he couldn't take care of it. What, what—what, what's another reason? Those are good reasons. What else do you think? What else? *(Laugh.)*

Thinking he never learned, right? That he was just a big boss? He was. Yeah, he was. Most people say, well, economically, he couldn't afford it. And that is true. You know, Thomas Jefferson died a hundred seven thousand dollars in debt. Many of his slaves were mortgaged, so he didn't have the right to sell them, but, oh, I mean to *free* them, but also, Thomas Jefferson said, he said, "You know, to free people brought up in the habits of slavery is like abandoning children."

Remember that law of 1806? When they had to leave within a year? That, uh played a big part in his decision, too. He just said until America is ready, these slaves can't be free. We all have to agree. You know, in his *Notes on the State of Virginia*—Now some of us might say, well, that's kind of a cop-out by Thomas Jefferson, but in his *Notes on the State of Virginia*, he had a *plan*, and his plan was . . . Eh, I think he sort of set the *year*, December 31, 1800, he said, Let's everybody . . . He said, By then, this is the age of the Enlightenment, *every*body will agree slavery is wrong, and by that year, let's take all the new babies born that year, we're gonna separate 'em from their mother and father. He said, I know that's gonna be hard, but, we've got to do it. And he said, The government's gonna pay. And we're going to train them, according, he said, to their genius. In trades. Then, when the women reach eighteen and the men twenty-one, we're going to take them, lock, stock, and barrel, and place them in a black community, maybe in the West Indies. Or maybe back to Africa. 'Cause he said, um, they will never forgive us for what ha— the, the way we treated them.

So, we will start trading. They, they'll have their own little country, we'll pay until they're ready. Okay, that was his plan. He was so disappointed when he, by 1800, you know, nobody's ready to do it. One of his friends, Edmund Coves, writes him, and he says, Now listen, I'm leavin' Virginia, and I'm freeing my slaves, and you ought to be the example. You ought to do the same thing.

He said, No. He said, I'm so sorry you have to leave Virginia. But he said, I just cannot abandon, you know, my family. He knew the time would come, and he felt that eventually everyone would agree, but until that time came, he said I wouldn't do it.

But, you know, too, the first forty years of his life, he speaks out against slavery. The last forty years, he gets real quiet.

Also (Thomas Jefferson) said about the slaves, he said, "Justice is in one scale and self-preservation in the other."

Now, one thing Abraham Lincoln said, that sort of clears it up a little bit for me, 'cause I get kind of mad at Thomas Jefferson, you know, for not being the example, but Abraham Lincoln said, "All praise to Jefferson." 'Cause he said, in the Declaration, Thomas Jefferson said, "Life, Liberty, and the Pursuit of Happiness," and he didn't put the word "property" in there?

Abraham Lincoln said if he had "property," and Thomas Jefferson knew this, if he had put that word "property" in, that Abraham Lincoln wouldn't have had this document that says, legally, "All—men—are—created—equal." You know, therefore, they should be free. And he said, "Because of Thomas Jefferson's foresight . . ."

Any questions 'bout that?

Slide: II. Cohabitation

Slide: The Sally Hemings Story

Slide: Ken Burns, Filmmaker

"James Callender"

(KEN BURNS *is seated in a rocking chair.*)

(*In reality a white male in his late thirties or forties. Boyish-looking.*)

You know what the Sally Hemings story is about?
Jefferson, hired newspapermen—
He said to Madison
"Hire people, who will *savage* Hamilton and Adams without
    letup
to *savage* them in the newspapers.
Callender, who was an alcoholic
(which is not a condition unfamiliar with those in our nation's
    capital),
turned *against* Jefferson
and wrote in a *Federalist* newspaper
his story about Sally Hemings.
No one's ever proved it, no one's ever disproved it.

Slide: James Callender, Journalist

The Recorder Newspaper, 1803

(CALLENDER *is at a nineteenth-century writing desk, writing by candlelight, in a vest and drinking from a bottle. He speaks with a thick Scottish brogue.*)

It is well known, that the man, whom it delighteth the people to honor, keeps and for many years past has kept, as his concubine, one of his own slaves.

Her name is Sally. The name of her eldest son is *Tom*. The boy is ten or twelve years of age. His features are said to bear a striking (although *sable*) resemblance to those of the President himself.

Other information assures us that Mr. Jefferson's Sally and her children are real persons, that the woman herself has a *room* to herself in Monticello in the character of seamstress to the family, if not as housekeeper; that she is industrious and orderly in her behavior, but that her intimacy with her master is well known. (CALLENDER *puts on a skirt, that is Sally Hemings's skirt, drinks, sings, and dances. Sings to the tune of "Yankee Doodle."*)

> *Of all the damsels in the green*
> *on mountain or in valley,*
> *A lass so luscious ne'er was seen,*
> *As Monticellan Sally!*
>
> *You call her slave, and pray were slaves*
> *Made only for the galley?*
> *Try for yourselves, ye witless knaves,*
> *And take to be your Sally.*

Slide: Roger Kennedy, Scholar/Historian/Author and Annette Gordon-Reed, Legal Scholar/Author

"Unconsummated Affections/Deep Denial"

Slide: A constructed dialogue: These people said these words but not in each other's presence.

(This should be played by one person who goes back and forth, playing both KENNEDY *and* REED. KENNEDY-REED *crosses center stage and sits on stool for the following debate.* KENNEDY *with a coffee cup and* REED *with a mimosa.)*

(In reality KENNEDY *is a middle-aged white male with extremely precise speech and a deep voice. Sitting in a sunny breakfast room. In reality* ANNETTE GORDON-REED *is a black woman in her late thirties or early forties with braids. She speaks very quickly and with confidence. Sitting in a hotel bar.)*

ROGER KENNEDY: I think Jefferson wasn't,
I think Jefferson,
as a man of words and unconsummated
a-ffections,
AAh,
there's just
not a *shred*,
not a *shred* of evidence . . .

Slide: Annette Gordon-Reed, Legal Scholar and Author of Thomas Jefferson and Sally Hemings.

ANNETTE GORDON-REED: Well that's crazy.

ROGER KENNEDY: That *before* his wife,
or *after* his wife there was anybody
with whom he was intimate
physically.
ANNETTE GORDON-REED: Well that's crazy.
ROGER KENNEDY: I just think,
I I don't I don't think it's necessary.
ANNETTE GORDON-REED: That's not true.
That's the asexual idea.
That is just—untrue.
And when somebody says something like that they can say the
    evidence doesn't convince them,
but to say there's no evidence,
that person is,
not a shred,
in deep denial.
And that person has to sit back
and think,
What is it about
this story that bothers you because you're not dealing realisti-
    cally
with it.
"There's not a shred."
It may not be enough to convince people, it's enough to
    convince
me,
it would convince people about any other guy in the world,
any other slave owner in the world,
it would be no question about it,
with what I've presented,
you can say it's not enough to convince you
but to say there's not a shred of evidence is just wrong, it's just
    flat
—wrong.

ROGER KENNEDY: Here are the signs and signals:
That there is this succession of young men
(quite handsome all of them),
that were his secretaries,
a gay friend of mine thinks this is *terribly* exciting
ANNETTE GORDON-REED: I haven't seen it written anywhere,
but there's a suggestion that
well
maybe
maybe he was gay.
Maybe,
that's why he,
never got married again
after
his wife died.
And I was joking with someone about this
I said, it's sort of like
pick your nightmare,
for historians.
I mean it's like if there's any intimation that he was *gay*
somebody will pick up the Sally Hemings story just like that.
(*Snapping her fingers.*)
Oh, but she was the love of his life,
it's like which is worse to be involved with a black woman or be
        gay?
The problem with the gay angle is, as I say—
if you don't have something
any indication that he had—
sex with
men,
but we need a name or an instance or something that indicates
        that
before you can have that as a realistic alternative

to this.

You see what I'm saying?

ROGER KENNEDY: I don't care, in a sense.

He surrounded himself with beautiful people.

Mostly male 'cause that's safe!

And where the hell are you gonna get a beautiful female to have
around if you're not married to her in Virginia?

ANNETTE GORDON-REED: I mean anything is possible

the other thing is,

that he masturbated.

Some people say well how do you know he wasn't just mastur-
     bating

all this time.

That that's how he—

I mean there are any number of—

I mean he could have been doing anything—

Masturbating,

there are people who thought he just masturbated and that's
     how he—

People have said this

people talk about it.

Historians surmise that.

ROGER KENNEDY: I think it's

only *sad*

Because the chances that they ever got anywhere

together

are just

zero.

No,

I just think he was

in *love*.

I mean he was *lonesome*.

I mean we all get *lonesome*.

ANNETTE GORDON-REED: This is a story
about a family of people
whether it's Jefferson or not
and these people were shut out of that family
because of
race.

(SALLY'S *rocker is being lit while actor/actress is entering as* JEF-
FERSON.)

Slide: Cinder Stanton, Historian at Monticello

"On Sally Hemings"

(ANNA DEAVERE SMITH's *voice is heard.*)

(*In the original production, the actual tape of the interview was used. Here a tape could be created with actors.*)

ANNA DEAVERE SMITH V.O.: And then again I mean we have no doc — there are no documents from her am I right about that?

CINDER STANTON: Right, nothing.

ANNA DEAVERE SMITH: Nothing at all?

CINDER STANTON: Nothing at all. No image, no documents.

ANNA DEAVERE SMITH: Was she literate — do we know that?

CINDER STANTON: We don't even know that. We know that, um . . .

ANNA DEAVERE SMITH: She could speak French though, right? They taught her to speak French.

CINDER STANTON: Well, we — it's an assumption. There's no record that she was given lessons, there's no record that, um, she knew it but you know it's a pretty strong assumption.

Slide: Scientific Evidence 1781–1998

Slide: From the Notes on the State of Virginia

(A *blackboard is brought onstage.* THOMAS JEFFERSON *dons a beautiful eighteenth-century waistcoat and asks for two crew members [one white, one black] to come onstage to assist his demonstration.*)

THOMAS JEFFERSON: The first difference which strikes us is that of colour.

Whether the black of the Negro resides in the reticular membrane between the skin and the scarf skin, or in the scarf skin itself, whether it proceeds from the colour of the bile, or from that of some other secretion, the difference is fixed in nature.

Are not the fine mixtures of red and white,

preferable to that eternal monotony, that immovable veil of black which covers all the motions of the other race?

They have less hair on the face and body.

They secrete less by the kidneys and more by the glands of the skin, which gives them a very strong and disagreeable odor. They are more ardent after their female,

but love seems with them to be a more eager desire, than a tender delicate mixture of sentiment and sensation.

In general, their existence appears to participate more of sensation than reflection.

Comparing them with their faculties of memory they are equal to whites, in reason much inferior, and in imagination they are dull, tasteless, and anomalous.

Never could I find that a black had uttered a thought above the level of plain narration.

Their inferiority is not the effect merely of their condition of life. I advance it therefore as a suspicion only, that the blacks whether originally a distinct race, or made distinct by time and circumstance, are inferior to the whites in the endowments of body and mind.

This unfortunate difference of colour, and perhaps of faculty is a powerful obstacle to the emancipation of these people.

When freed he is to be removed beyond the reach of mixture.

(JEFFERSON *approaches the blackboard and writes on it.*)

Slide: From Correspondence of Thomas Jefferson

JEFFERSON: You asked me in conversation, what constituted a mulatto by our law? It becomes a mathematical problem.

Let the first crossing be of a, pure Negro, with A, pure white. The unit of blood of the issue being composed of the half of that of each parent, will be a/two + A/two. Call it, for abbreviation, b (half blood).

Let q and e cohabit, the half of the blood of each will be q/two + e/two = a/eight + A/eight + B/four + a/sixteen + A/sixteen + B/eight + C/four = a(3)/sixteen + A(3)/sixteen + B(3)/eight + C/four, wherein 3/sixteen of a is no longer a mulatto. Our canon considers two crosses with the pure white, as clearing the issue of the Negro blood.

But observe, that this does not reestablish freedom, which depends on the condition of the mother. So much for this trifle by way of correction.

"Could Have Not Had Our Mess as Bad"

The cohabitation is palpable.
When you're in that bed
and in that room
and the
smell and *sound* of black people is absolutely the first thing that
hits you in the morning—
Every laugh,
Every salacious comment,
Every,
what you're having for breakfast,
it's right where that pond is!
Right there!
It's that close!
The guy serving your *tea*
is your
nephew
really.
That's, just
that's
that that that you can,
that's very *rough*.
Torture I think.
The obscenity is
that very few who got so interested in it
were interested in all those redheaded kids
running around Monticello.
Nobody paid any attention to *them*

until they got interested in the possibility that
Mr. *Tom*
had produced a baby
with a black woman
when the place was *teeming* with kids
produced with black women.
We are talking about *scores*
of children produced in a power relationship.
He lived in a *swarm* of children conceived in power relation-
      ships,
that were unacceptable to any moral person.
Instead of being *mad* at him
which is easy.
This is somebody who lived
for a —
until *eighty*
knowing
that he was living every day in moral ambiguity.
Everything he did, had a shadow side to it.
In 1806 there was a very large congressional debate about
      whether
slaves
were to go into the Louisiana Purchase or not
and Jefferson
who
who had done *nothing* since 1784
to make it harder for slavery to spread into the west—
nothing
found it convenient not to have his acquisition free.
Everything after that, Missouri and all the rest of it
flowed from a *failure* to
stop it when it could have been stopped.
It isn't true

that we didn't have another chance!
So we could—have—not—had—our—mess
as bad.
Yeah.
To me *that's* the story.

Slide: Eugene Foster, Author of the 1998 report on DNA of Jefferson and the Descendants of Sally Hemings

"Probability"

(In reality a white male, a scientist.)

Our uh,
scientific results did not prove,
that Thomas Jefferson
fathered any of Sally Hemings's children.
But that
the information that we got
taken in the context of the best available historical information
makes it extremely likely.
I think that the general public does not understand that.
I think that the general public uh has come to believe that
the DNA evidence
has proved the relationship.
We absolutely cannot say that.
I emphasized strongly
and in a *loud* voice—
I emphasized strongly
that it would not be possible
for us to prove
anything
with one hundred percent certainty
either positively or negatively.
I have long understood
that the whole idea of probability is
something that most people just

don't understand.
If you say well this is very likely
uh,
that's something people don't want
to deal with.
They want to know is it? Or isn't it?
What one can say in summary, is that this has tipped the weight
    of
evidence very strongly in favor of the interpretation
that Thomas Jefferson
is more likely,
the father.

Slide: Ken Burns, Filmmaker

"Teacup"

(KEN BURNS *is in the rocking chair stage right.*)

It doesn't matter.
He *owned* her.
Get the story straight.
I mean he could have *killed* her if he wanted.
He *owned* her!
He could have done *anything* with her!
He could have *murdered* her—
They could have said, "Mr. President, where's Sally?"
And he could have said, "Oh I killed her last night, she
    displeased me," and there wasn't a law in the land that
could have touched him.
The fact of whether he did or he didn't,
this late twentieth-century obsession with all things
sexual, titillating, and celebrity-driven is anathema to historical
    truth.
He *owned* her and we forget that fact, but the fact that
the man—who—authored—the—world's—words—which—
    we—consider—our—*creed*
held in chattel slavery more than two hundred human beings
one of whom
was a young, and we are told attractive and potentially *lover* for
him, but it doesn't matter the sexual politics are overwhelmed
by the fact that he *owned* her!
I like the frisson that comes from
both sides—

"Yes of course he could have" but no he absolutely didn't!
But he *owned* her goddamn it
that's the point he *owned* her!
And that's what we forget—
And we go, "yes yes yes"
I say, "Okay
so can I tell you about slavery?"
I said,
"Would you like to live
in a one-room dirt-floored shack fourteen by fourteen in which
    you work fourteen hours a day—
unless there is a full moon and then you work more, you are not
    paid,
you can be beaten, you can be separated from your family. In
    fact
they changed the wedding vows for slaves to read "Till death or
    distance do you part." *(Slight pause.)*
You are susceptible to every known disease of which there is no
    cure, you are denied the possibility of an education and in
    fact,
in many instances you would be punished for learning a lan-
    guage or having a literature or having a culture.
Now tell me how long you would like to live under this?"
I would say a generation's too long.
A decade's too long, a year is too long.
A month is too long, a week's too long.
I submit if you were asked to do that
you might try it on for twenty minutes.
That's—
He *owned* her.
You know if I own you—
When I say he could have killed her—
You say,

"Hell yes, but he wouldn't have."

His—nephews—murdered—one—of—his—slaves

and their, that slave's crime had been to break a *teacup* that had
belonged to their mother!

And there—was—no—recourse—in—the—United—States—
of—America.

He's both the blessing and the curse.

As John Hope Franklin said,

He, he ensured, that we would inherit the poison of indecision
on race.

And yet he also wrote us the prescription for the antidote.

For the serum that would cure us.

Jefferson said that slavery was like holding a wolf by the ears,
you

didn't like it but you didn't dare let go.

Slide: III. An Easier Time

Slide: R. W. Apple, Journalist for The New York Times

"At All, At All, At All, At All"

(Sound: Restaurant ambience, laughter. APPLE *is in an Indian restaurant in Washington, D.C., near the White House, very upscale. He is drinking white wine. White linens and fine china are on the table. He wears a napkin at his neck and is eating Indian hors d'oeuvres. In reality he is a large white man, wearing a tie, blazer, penny loafers, with a deep vocal register. He is surveying the menu with reading glasses.)*

But uh Roosevelt, Roosevelt conducted press conferences with reporters standing around his desk. But my God, what a change since—in the relatively short time between FDR and now. You know, the famous story about Bob Post? There was a reporter called Robert *Post* on *The New York Times* and who was later killed in a bombing raid over Wilhelmshaven. I think—check it if you use it—during the war. But when he was a young reporter, and he came from a rather grand family like Roosevelt. And he asked an unanswer—— an unanswerable question, an *unaskable* question to wit, "Are—you—going—to—run—for—a—third—term?" And Roosevelt said, *(Pronounce long and slow.)* "Bob, put your dunce cap on and go stand in the corner." Now, this is *not* something that would—could happen today. At all, at all, at all, at all! And there are no unaskable questions now, as was demonstrated with the, Gary *Hart* question in New *Hampshire.* Ya know, you've just, you've gone from presuming what the President says is true and unthinking, unthinking backing of a wartime emer-

gency, to presuming what the Presidents say is *un*true. And we've gone from credulousness, through what I would see as a relatively healthy period of of skepticism, to what I see now as a relatively *un*healthy period of cynicism. And what, what bothers me—
(Waiter enters.)

If I order—if I were to order the shrimp curry, could you make it a bit *hot*? So I won't—I need a bit of heat in this—in the hot weather. What you just—what do you think you'd like?

Slide: The Roosevelt White House: "A Family"

Slide: Walter Trohan, White House Correspondent for the Chicago Tribune *from FDR to Nixon*

"An Easier Time"

(In reality a ninety-three-year-old white male with very poor vision shuffling toward an easy chair, wearing jacket and tie.)

The only reason I'm talking to you is to give you a feeling of a
  period
of an easier time
a friendlier time
when I had associations that reporters can't have today,
as I say
 we were a *family*.
We would have *parties* for Roosevelt and put on little *shows* for
  'im
we'd sing *songs* and write little skits and so forth.
We did different things and
he would—
Ohhhhhh
we'd pretend ta,
oh *God*,
imitate Shirley Temple for example who was popular at that
  time
in uh
some silly song or other.
And he enjoyed that kind of nonsense.
And we'd have drinks of course. . . .

Slide: Lizzie McDuffie, Former White House Cook for FDR

"Canary Bird"

Slide: Voice of Bernard Asbell, Historian, and Lizzie McDuffie, Former White House Cook for FDR

(BERNARD ASBELL *was a white man who interviewed* LIZZIE MCDUFFIE *in the fifties or sixties. He sounds like a fastidious historian who lives for details.* LIZZIE MCDUFFIE, *in reality, almost got cast as the role that Hattie McDaniel played in* Gone with the Wind, *and sounds like it. She seems slightly intimidated by* ASBELL. ASBELL's *voice should be prerecorded, or done on a God mike. In the original production, the actual tape of* ASBELL *was used. Here a tape could be created with actors. He should not be seen.* MCDUFFIE *is making biscuits.*)

VOICE OF BERNARD ASBELL: This is going to be an interview with Mrs. Lizzie McDuffie, and we've just started to talk right now. Do you recall, say on the morning of April twelfth . . . maybe if I began with a question that I was wondering—
LIZZIE MCDUFFIE: (*Making biscuits center stage.*) Yes, that will help me because uh
VOICE OF BERNARD ASBELL: Do you mind if I smoke a cigarette?
LIZZIE MCDUFFIE: Oh no! Help yourself by all means.
VOICE OF BERNARD ASBELL: Do you know what he usually had—what—what do you, what would you guess he had on his breakfast tray that morning? Was there any—
LIZZIE MCDUFFIE: Uh
well,
Mr. Roosevelt was very fond of fish.
He was a man that he likedded [*sic*] broiled fish.

He, he liked-ed fish
he, he ate well.
And sometimes he had scrambled eggs and bacon.
He liked bacon.
He always said that the bacon,
uh you shouldn't,
couldn't use a knife and a fork with bacon and fried chicken.
You had to eat it with your fingers.
He said he always would—
the bacon would fly off your plate and then you
you'd miss your bacon.
VOICE OF BERNARD ASBELL: Well now, as far as you can
remember
on that morning,
uh the routine was as usual.
(LIZZIE *begins reading from her diary, unbound, handwritten*
sheets.)
That morning while I was getting the sitting room in order,
Mr. Roosevelt called to me and said
uh oh
Lizzie, Lizzie says uh
"You all were havin' a grand time this morning a grand time!"
And I said uh
"What do you mean, Mr. Roosevelt?"
He said, "Well, I heard all that laughter out there."
I said, "Oh my, I wondered,
did we disturb you?
I'm awful sorry."
"Oh no no no I enjoy
laughter," he says.
"There's nothing in the world that fills me up like laughter," he
said.
"The world needs more laughter."
And I said,

"Well
you, do you
Mr. Roosevelt
are you, um
do you believe in
oh what is that word?
Do you . . ."
(LIZZIE *looks on her paper.*)
It's on here.
Do you do you . . .
VOICE OF BERNARD ASBELL: That's all right . . .
LIZZIE MCDUFFIE: *(She laughs.)*
I stammer so . . .
"Do you believe in reincarnation?"
VOICE OF BERNARD ASBELL: Oh! Reincarnation.
LIZZIE MCDUFFIE: And he said,
"Do I believe in what?"
I said, "Reincarnation."
He said, "Do you believe in reincarnation?"
I said, "I don't know whether I do or not I say," but I said,
    "That's what Joe was trying to find out this morning."
Joe was the Filipino butler that we had carried down to help out
    with
us
uh on that trip.
And I says uh, "He wants to know if I believe in reincarnation."
I said, "I don't know whether I believe in it or not
but
in case there is such a thing as reincarnation
when I come back I want to be a canary bird."
He looked at me from head to foot and I weighed about two
    hundred pounds then and he bursts out into *peals* of
    laughter.

And he had a favorite word that he always said when anything
    amused him.
He said, "Don't you love it don't you love it!??"
That was—
VOICE OF BERNARD ASBELL: Whenever he was happy . . .
LIZZIE MCDUFFIE: Oh yes.
Oh, that's the way he expressed himself.
Don't you love it? Don't you love it?!!!!
And I said,
"Well
(She takes more papers out of her apron pocket.)
I hope
I
will come back
and be a canary bird."
Then let's see what else
there was something else that was said.
Oh goodness
I think after you are gone I'll think of everything.
Well . . .

Slide: Walter Trohan, White House Correspondent for the Chicago Tribune *from FDR to Nixon*

"How Could You Say It"

Personally,
he was charming.
He had charisma.
But I didn't like his private life.
I must say
he brought his mistress into the White House
ANNA DEAVERE SMITH V.O.: Why didn't anybody write about
    that?
(Pause.)
WALTER TROHAN: . . . because she was so nice.
And if anybody mentioned it to me
and said she was the mistress and whatnot
I'd say,
"You got a dirty mind."
(Pause. Considering.)
She
was in
love with the guy
and she was a charming person
and she was crazy about him.
I was sympathetic
toward her.
I didn't think it was the right thing for him to do *(angrily)*
and then he *disgusted* me completely
and I was very angry,
privately,

when
when he got playin' around with Crown Princess Margaret.
It broke (Missy's) heart
and she got very *ill*
went into Doctor's hospital
and Roosevelt
called on her *once*!
And ya know what he did?
He took his *wife* with him.
And I thought the *idea* of takin' the wife to see your *discarded
    mistress*
because you were *ashamed* to go in there alone
it rather disgusted me.
ANNA DEAVERE SMITH V.O.: But you never wrote about it?
WALTER TROHAN: I *couldn't* (write) about it.
I couldn't say she was his mistress —
because she was in the White House as the secretary —
and everybody knew she was the mistress —
but how could you say it?
They could have *blasted* me and I would have been a terrible
character.
Well I don't know
I don't think my paper would have printed it.
Actually, ya know he wasn't functioning for the last year or so.
He was ill
I knew he was dyin',
his own doctor said he was healthy.
I knew there was
things were goin' on
so
I knew he was having doctors come in.
I was his, I tell ya I'm a reporter, and I
enlisted

got another reporter,
and the two of us brought a doctor
and sat him at a White House dinner,
White House Correspondents' Dinner
within a few feet of Roosevelt
to watch 'im and tell 'em how he was go—— what he thought of
    him.
And then after the dinner
I said, "Well how was he?"
He says, "He's a dyin' man."

Slide: Michael K. Frisby, Journalist for The Wall Street Journal

"Bowling"

(In reality a black man in his forties, conservatively dressed.)

And, now, fast forward into the White House. Okay?
George—Bush—is—always—inviting— Now, I didn't
cover Bush,* but I heard stories. He'd invite reporters over
for little *chats.* He'd go *bowling,* bring them over for *bowling.*
Yeah, there's a bowling alley down in the White House:
He'd bring them over for—in the studio to see
movies with him and stuff. Okay?
Now, what I'll say is, I don't think that got him
favorable *stories.* Okay?
But what it *did* get him was benefit of the doubt.
Okay?
What I think that got him was when, whenever there was a issue
    of, "Okay, who do I believe here? Do I believe George
    Bush? Or do I believe somebody else?"
I think he got the benefit of the doubt from these
people because they knew him, they got to know him.
    (Singsong.)
They liked him.
I think they probably gave him the benefit of the doubt on some
    things. Okay?
Bill Clinton *never* gets the benefit of the doubt because he has
kep'—us—at—such—a—distance.
Okay?

*Ed. note: referring to George Hebert Bush

He has never let us *in*.
He has never let—
I mean I've,
I've gotten in by kind of *prying* and just,
you know,
making sure that I always keep my eye on this guy.
Okay?
That's how I've gotten to have a bit of an *understanding* with
him.
Okay?
But he hasn't made it *easy*, because I'd get *rare* opportunities.
Okay?
I think I've been to what?
I've been to like one dinner in the White House in five years?
I work for *The Wall Street Journal*.
Okay?
(*Lowering his voice*.)
I've never been to the bowling alley.
Heh, heh.
Okay?
If he cuddled—if he cuddled up to us, he'd start getting benefit
of the doubt.
Oh, I don't.
Look, look, look.
They may *tell* you that shit?
You going to tell me
that my colleagues wouldn't like to go *bowling* at the White
House *bowling* alley with the President of the United
States?
You going to tell me
that my colleagues wouldn't like to go over and see a *movie* with
the President and the First Family?
Okay?

Now, not that I'm saying it would have any effect at all on *news*
    coverage.
Okay?
But if you were faced with a situation where you have to decide
    who you're going to believe, Bill Clinton or somebody else,
    and you've gotten to know this Bill Clinton a little bit and
    you suddenly start thinking that,
"Well, you know, he's got substance.
He's got a little more structure than I thought."
You might give him the benefit of the doubt!
That's where I think the President could benefit.
By the press knowing him a little more.
Okay?
And I'll tell you my personal?
I'm willing to bet that it would relate to a lot of other people.
Okay?
If I get a picture of me bowling with the President and I send
    that to my mom or I send that to my aunts or I send that to
    my godmother, they're happy as all get-out, because when
    their friends come to the house, they can say,
"Look!
There's Michael *bowling* with the President of the
United States."
Okay?

Slide: Lizzie McDuffie, Former White House Cook for FDR

"Hot Water Bottle/Peeved"

(Reading from her sheets of paper, expressively, as if reading to a group of children.)

When—I—asked—him—that—morning—how—he—felt
he says,
"I don't feel any . . .
"I don't feel any too good this mornin'
Lizzie."
And he threw his hand right back there.
Just like that. *(She throws her hand back, imitating.)*
I was in the guest cottage
tidying up when Arthur came in and asked for a hot water
     bottle.
I got the hot *(Uncertainly, unable to read her writing.)*
got the hot hot water bottle
and gave it, gave it to him.
And in a few minutes Daisy came down and said, "Lizzie, why
     hadn't you come, why hadn't you come down?" *(With emo-
     tion, as that person, very good performance.)*
And I said, "It isn't—the lunch is not ready yet.
It isn't lunchtime!"
And I said, "What happened?"
And she said, "Oh Lizzie, I believe the President is dying." *(Very
     good performance of that person, with feeling.)*
That was when I just *flew* to pieces!
That's when I said,
"Why didn't you tell me?

Why didn't he tell me that the President was sick?"
And then I thought to myself—
Oh how much I *loved* him and how I waited on him all this
    time
and then Arthur would come *(Exasperated, angry.)*
and *know* he was sick
and wouldn't even tell me.
I was peeved about that
I remember having that, feeling like that about it.

Slide: Gary Hart, Candidate for President, 1988

"Look in Windows"

(In reality a middle-aged white male: on the telephone.)

I think it's much more profound than just
the press and people's private lives.
I think it's a real issue of control.
I think what
political journalism in the late twentieth century wants is
     control.
I think it wants to use its access,
its intrusiveness
to to control—
to have more control of the process,
political process.
And it also comes about in my case.
For example saying, "When Hart was driven from the race."
I *wasn't* driven from the race.
I chose not to move forward.
It was *my* choice.
So that's the issue:
What—is—the—meaning—of—language?
It's: What is the power, what is the control of the political
     process?
I think that's what the Gary Hart issue is about.
It wasn't about sex
or scandal.
It was about power.
Who—decides—who—will—run—for—office—in—this—
     country?

That's what it's about.
And who decides what is moral and immoral?
And how do you know what goes on in someone's house?
How do you know what goes on in someone's personal life?
You *can't*.
You *can't*.
That's—the—simple—point.
You can speculate.
You can spy.
You can look in windows.
You can sensationalize.
You can use gossip.
But you will never,
never
know.

"Asylum"

I'm not sure this is going to make any sense but since it may,
    let's try it.
You remember in the eighteenth century,
in the eighteenth and nineteenth century
in the finer and more refined circles in England
it became *habit* to go to um,
homes for the mentally ill and go see the people there and be
    very *moved* by their predicament?
It was a *weird*
sort of thing—
You wanted to go see the mad people and then feel.
Then I'm going to show all your friends,
"See how compassionate I am.
I'm deeply *moved*
by their misery.
I am deeply *moved*
by the misery around me.
Then again I've always been very sensitive!"
The—*press*—is—the—*exact*—opposite—of—that.
They, they don't—they want to go to the insane asylum and
    make the crazy people *cry*!
They want to go to the insane asylum with a *fork* and say, "Hey,
    how'd you like *that*, Dole?"
(Makes a gesture: sticking the fork.)
"Hey Clinton,
what did you mean about, Susan McDougal and her

and her uh legal bills?"
I love to see old 1930s films of,
you know 1930s old tape
of the great ocean liner landing in New York and Greta Garbo
    gets off and, you know, says hello to her *fans*?
You know those old arrival
shipping news kind of videos from Movietone?
Do you remember the one with the Queen and King of En-
    gland coming down the *plank*?
And some, some of the photographers start yelling, "Hey Queen
    this way!"
That's what journalism is,
at its worst and still at its best!
"Hey—Queen—look—this—way.—Hey—King—over—
    here"—click—click.

Slide: IV. The Grand Deaths of the Race

(If done by one actor, he/she wears LINCOLN'S *shoes for all charac-*
ters.)

(Note: This section should feel like a kind of physical "jazz." If
played by one actor, it should feel as though that actor were wan-
dering through a variety of other people's dreams, or from one
sideshow to the next at a carnival. Music should play behind the
entire section. The play Our American Cousin *should have a*
sound design, which becomes more and more overpowering and
grotesque as the act unfolds. The microphone should echo,
enhance, or distort Whitman from time to time. If more than one
actor performs this section, it should seem that one actor flows to
the next seamlessly—as if they are all disjointed parts of the same
story. If more than one actor is used, the actor playing LINCOLN
should also play PALMER.*)*

Slide: The Lincoln White House

Slide: Elizabeth Keckley, former slave, dressmaker to Mrs. Lincoln

(The stage is set up with a dressmaker's model stage left. A
nineteenth-century coffin is center stage. LINCOLN'S *rocker from*
Ford's Theater is stage right.)

ELIZABETH KECKLEY: My name is Elizabeth Keckley. My life has
been an eventful one. I was born a slave—was the child of slave
parents. The twelve hundred dollars with which I purchased the
freedom of myself and son I consented to accept only as a loan. I

went to work in earnest, and in a short time paid every cent. Ever since arriving in Washington I had a great desire to work for the ladies of the White House. One day when I was very busy, one of my patrons drove up to my apartment, came in where I engaged with my needle, and said: "I know Mrs. Lincoln well, and you shall make a dress for her." It appears that Mrs. Lincoln had upset a cup of coffee on the dress.

I crossed the threshold of the White House for the first time. I became the regular dressmaker of Mrs. Lincoln. *(Music. A loud clock.)*

Slide: President Abraham Lincoln

"Lincoln's Dream"
From a letter written by Abraham Lincoln

(Sitting in a rocking chair, dressed in a long black coat and top hat, using a microphone which should have some effect, as an echo, a reverb, et cetera. Music.)

About ten days ago, I retired very late. I had been up waiting for important dispatches from the front. I could not have been long in bed when I fell into a slumber, for I was weary. I soon began to dream. There seemed to be a deathlike stillness about me. Then I heard subdued sobs, as if a number of people were weeping. I thought I left my bed and wandered downstairs. There the silence was broken by the same pitiful sobbing, but the mourners were invisible. I went from room to room; no living person was in sight, but the same mournful sounds of distress met me as I passed along.

I saw light in all the rooms; every object was familiar to me; but where were all the people who were grieving as if their hearts would break? I was puzzled and alarmed. What could be the meaning of all this?

Determined to find the cause of a state of things so mysterious and so shocking, I kept on until I arrived at the East Room, which I entered.

There I met with a sickening surprise. Before me was a catafalque, on which rested a corpse wrapped in funeral vestments. Around it were stationed soldiers who were acting as guards; and there was a throng of people, gazing mournfully upon the corpse, whose face was covered, others weeping pitifully. "Who is dead in the White House?" I demanded of one of the soldiers. "The President," was his answer; "he was killed by an assassin."

Then came a loud burst of grief from the crowd, which woke me from my dream. I slept no more that night; and although it was only a dream, I have been strangely annoyed by it ever since.

"Body Watch"

("Stars and Stripes Forever" plays)

(PALMER *in Lincoln's jacket and shoes, dons a baseball cap, on backwards.* [PALMER *is in reality a black man.*] *He crosses upstage of coffin to retrieve his photo bag, circles the stage with his light meter scoping the sight during the following speech.* PALMER *brings photo bag down left.*)

Like so many things in the journalistic realm these days
that's kind of market driven,
so
your competitors are there,
so you have to be there.
And if this cataclysmic event
actually does happen and your representative isn't there
to photograph it or to tape it, or to get firsthand color
then um you're, you're, you're blown out of the water,
on
hour fifteen
of uh a Clinton
hour fifteen
of a Presidential trip to ya-know-*x*-state
when you're tromping through the thirty-seventh factory
of the day
and hearing the same boilerplate speech
it does feel a little bit like you're just there

to,
watch the body.
And see,
you know and and and to to to you know cover your organiza-
    tion or *protect* (in the Washington lingo)
your organization in case
the unmentionable happens.
The unmentionable?
I mean just in case POTUS
gets, you know, POTUS gets *waxed*.
Oh right.
PRESIDENT—OF—THE—UNITED—STATES.

Slide: Walt Whitman, Journalist/Poet

"President of the United States"

(1865. WHITMAN *is standing stage right of coffin at a standing microphone with a bunch of lilacs in his hand. He is dressed like* LINCOLN, *except no top hat.)*

The grand deaths of the race,
The dramatic deaths of every
nationality are its most
important inheritance — in some
respects beyond its literature
and art.
How often my heart has entertained the wish,
to give of Abraham Lincoln's death
its own special memorial.
The season being advanced,
there were many lilacs in full bloom. I find myself always
    reminded of the great tragedy of that day by the
sight and odor of these blossoms.
The popular afternoon paper of Washington,
the little *Evening Star,*
had spattered all over its third page,
"THE PRESIDENT AND HIS LADY WILL BE AT THE
    THEATRE THIS
EVENING."
Lincoln was fond of the theater.
I have myself seen him there several times.
I remember thinking how funny it was that he,
in some respects the leading actor in the stormiest drama known
to real history's stage through centuries,

should sit there and be so completely interested
and absorbed in those human jack straws,
moving about with their silly little gestures,
foreign spirit and flatulent text.

(LINCOLN *makes an entrance; as into Ford's Theater. Musical fan-
fare, ovation, applause. He bows and bows, as the shadow of*
BOOTH *with a gun appears and the V.O. of the play begins.*)

Slide: From Our American Cousin, *a play performed at the
Ford's Theater in Washington the night Lincoln was shot*

MRS. M: *(A woman's British voice.)* As to the state of your affec-
tions, remember, your happiness for life will depend on the
choice you make.
AUGUSTA: *(A younger British woman's voice.)* What would you
advise, Mamma? You know I am always advised by you.

Slide: Ben Bradlee, * *Former Editor of* The Washington Post

"Performers"

(In reality a white, patrician man in his seventies, handsome, well-heeled, perfect physical shape.)

(Sitting at a desk with a swivel chair turned sideways.)

Well, it started with television, right?
It started with television.
These guys,
uh—they were really performers uh, uh, Brinkley
uh,
Cronkite,
Sevareid.
These were *performers* and uh, uh, it, it got so
that *what* they said
was less important than how they said it
and the authority that they could,
uh, force the public to believe they *had.*
And then as we got *used* to this,
as this became part of our *culture,*
they ceased to be reporters of any kind.
They're *not.*
But in this wonderful time
when we were downstairs in the city room,
when *Hoffman* was here,

*Ben Bradlee was the editor of *The Washington Post* when Watergate unfolded. The story broke on his watch. He is portrayed in *All the President's Men* by Jason Robards.

Dustin,
And he was absorbing,
and trying to learn how we all talked
and what the culture of—
and, you know, not unlike what,
I guess, what you're doing.
And we got the word that there was a *jumper.*
A jumper means that somebody has gone out a window and is
     threatening to jump into the street
and off himself.
I said to Dustin,
Would you—yeah, you want to see this?
This is a,
uh, a kind of a, uh, ritual story.
Happens twice a year
and happens to almost all reporters.
They get to cover it.
So,
we went down and walked and it was right around the corner.
We walked a block and a half.
And, you know, everybody's looking *up* this way and a few
     people
say, "Jump. Jump!"
But mostly just looking.
Then they spotted *Hoffman,*
and the whole audience turned around and looked at *us.*
Just, they all looked at *Hoffman!*
Now, if, if,
uh, *Dan Rather* did that;
he went to cover a jump,
they'd do the same thing.
They *intrude*—*(Louder, stronger.)*
upon the event

and this is why the smart editors
who taught us wanted us off the stage
because, uh, uh, you *changed*
the event by your presence if you're really a performer.
There's a principle in physics,
I have the book.
I bought this *huge* physics book,
which is so unusual for me,
called *The Heisenberg Principle*
and—and that is, if you,
if you, uh, split an atom,
you don't end up with two half atoms; *(Louder.)*
you end up with two different things!
Observing the phenomenon *changes* the phenomenon.

WHITMAN: And so the figure Booth, the murderer . . .

(The BOOTH *shadow appears.)*

Slide: From Our American Cousin, *performed the night of Lincoln's death.*

(The melodrama is very loud.)

MRS. M.: Augusta my dear, to your room!
AUGUSTA: Yes, Ma, The nasty beast.

Slide: Brian Palmer, Photographer/Journalist, Former Photographer for U.S. News and World Report

"Political Theater"

(PALMER *is loading film.*)

I hate to use a word as strong as "manipulation" but
essentially
I,
we are are are documenting political theater, I mean it's
it's
very elaborately staged political theater.
And it's the same under Republicans as it is under Democrats.
They're trying to get their message out with as little
interference and as little noise as possible.
Having to
document that is kind of difficult.
I mean just sitting in the van,
the conversations that go on oftentimes
among photographers are often
about missed pictures.
People who missed pictures.
So I mean you're ya know you're sort of really
imbued with this,
this knowledge from very early on.
Basically just like the Secret Service
you want to have the President *in* your viewfinder
or in your view
pretty much all the darn time.

Slide: Walt Whitman

(WHITMAN *is at the microphone.*)

WHITMAN: And in the midst of the pandemonium, infuriated
    soldiers, the audience and the crowd, the stage, and all its
    actors and actresses, its paint pots, spangles, and gaslights,
    the lifeblood from those veins, the best and sweetest of the
    land, drips slowly down and death's ooze already begins its
    little bubbles on the lips.

Slide: From Our American Cousin, *performed the night of Lincoln's death.*

(LINCOLN *sits and enjoys the play with laughter. The melodrama
below is very loud, grotesque. The shadow of* BOOTH *gets bigger and
bigger—gun is drawn slowly.*)

ASA: You crave affection, you do. Now I've no fortune, but I'm
    balling over with affections, which I'm ready to pour out all
    over you like apple sass, over roast pork.
MRS. M.: I am aware, Mr. Trenchard, you are not used to the
    manners of good society, and that, alone, will excuse the
    impertinence of which you have been guilty.
ASA: Don't know the manners of good society, eh? Well I guess I
    know enough to turn you inside out, old gal—you sockdol-
    ogizing old man trap.

(On "sockdologizing old man trap," *loud laughter on sound track
of entire theater audience. Gunshot.* LINCOLN *falls forward, hat
rolls, actor morphs into* BRIAN PALMER, *and starts taking pictures
madly. Strobe.*)

Slide: Gloria Steinem, Author/Activist

"Three Murders"

(Big chair comes onto center stage.)

(In reality an attractive white woman in her sixties who looks forty.)

I always felt sorry for Nixon,
you know,
because he should not have been President.
And if it had not been for three murders,
he wouldn't have been.
(Pause.)
He was a classic example of—
Two Kennedys and a Martin Luther King,
I mean, on the grounds that I—
Well, because I think if he had not been—
Because he was so much—
He and the movement were so much a bridge;
it was so focused on voting and the right to vote,
you know, and it was the bridge between—
a bridge between a giant populist movement for justice and the
system,
and when that bridge was gone,
I think it was very disillusioning and difficult.
But I don't mean to oversell, you know,
but it just—it always felt emotionally like it took three murders
to get him in office and he was clearly—
he had clearly risen to the level of his incompetence,
and he was a small man in a big office.

(Pause.)
But every time I got,
every time I felt sorry for him,
he always did something so
horrendous
that then I would . . .

Slide: Governor Ann Richards, Former Governor of Texas

"Birds That Were Loose"

(Sitting in an elegant chair. In reality a white woman in her sixties with beautiful white hair. Texas accent. Lots of volume, on the telephone.)

I'm gonna get my coffee.
So you have the picture here—
The country uh
feels good because of this man who who because of his
ability to speak well,
because he conveyed a sort of new mission—
The problem was that he had his uh detractors.
I would say that a segment of the white population
whites and Hispanics
were
very enthusiastic about Jack Kennedy.
But the establishment
uh-uh.
No.
There was a very strong right-wing movement
that we felt greatly in the state of Texas.
So when the decision was made for Kennedy,
When he made the decision was made to come to Texas
he was advised not—to—come.
Now, here's what was going on in Dallas.
There was a sort of a lunatic,
retired general
named Edwin Walker,

who lived out on Turtle Creek
that—
depending on what the government did at one time or another
flew his flag upside down,
because that was a military sign of distress.
So the day that Jack Kennedy came to town
or maybe the week before,
I remember a lot of talk about the fact
that Edwin Walker was flying his flag upside down.
Uh
Lyndon and Lady Bird Johnson had come to visit Dallas—
They um were going into the downtown hotel and there were a
bunch of Republican women,
all dressed up
hats and gloves and the whole—and
who were picketing
uh against Lyndon Johnson
and who
got carried away and *hit* Lady Bird,
and and Johnson
with their picket signs.
Just stupid, silly
juvenile
embarrassing
kinds of stuff.
It wan' pretty.
It was grown-up white boy games.
If you remember, in the old days—
well of course you don't remember—
There was no Republican Party.
You couldn't participate
unless you were a Democrat.
So what you had in the Democratic Party, were, Republicans.
So Kennedy made the decision he was going to come,

to try to heal—the—rift.
The luncheon was held in a place called the Apparel Mart—
Now this is,
this is interesting to me.
(She laughs.)
The Apparel Mart was a wholesale place,
and Dallas was really proud of it 'cause it was brand new,
with a big open atrium that went up about
four stories
and at that time I had about as much swat as a
flyswatter so
I think I was on the third balcony or something.
But here's the interesting thing—
in this hall there were,
parakeets.
Flying.
I mean,
Birds,
that were loose!
Yeah.
And that was supposed to be one of the charming attributes of
    the Apparel Mart.
(She laughs.)
And I kept thinking well
the birds
undoubtedly are gonna drop on our food.
I have not been back to the Apparel Mart since.
(She laughs.)
I have no idea what they did with the birdshit.
So
everybody's all dressed up.
Very very excited.
The
the reception

could *not* have been more enthusiastic.
I mean there were
people *everywhere*
all over the airport.
The streets of course were
were jammed.
And I read in the papers that Connally had turned to Kennedy,
and said, "Well, Mr. President, you certainly can't say that Texas
    doesn't love ya."
People had in the hall, where we were waiting for him for lunch
had portable radios
listening to his progress in the motorcade
so kind of the word would be whispered from one table to the
    next
what point the motorcade had reached
and we heard, someone with a radio, that something had hap-
    pened.
People on the floor I saw were running up to the front where all
the dignitaries—
We knew something was wrong.
Someone got to the podium
and I can't remember what they said,
the place was so buzzing
with people turning and looking and all kind of talking at once.
And something was said that that
the President had been shot.
And um
and I know my first instinct was I had to get home.
I think that was the first instinct of almost everyone there.
(Blackout.)

Intermission

Slide: ACT TWO

Slide: I. A Scream: The Clinton White House

Slide: Alice Waters, Chef, Chez Panisse Restaurant

"Presidential Peach"

(Downstage center, carrying a peach, wearing a knit cap. In reality she is a "hip," sophisticated, classy, white woman in her fifties from Berkeley, California.)

He did come to Chez Panisse.
(She giggles.)
Uhm
it was
electrifying for me.
I wanted him to
have a really good time here.
I knew I, that I couldn't make an impression on him in terms of
    food.
I knew that I couldn't
in that
in that period of time,
with just one time.
Because
uh uhm ah
I just think it's very hard for a public person
who doesn't eat well—
to immediately—
And I didn't want to force him into eating
what I wanted him to eat.
I put him in the back, behind the oven in the little corner
behind the booths,

and ate
every other tomato that I served him!
Just to make sure they were the most perfect tomatoes!
And he never ate one!
(She laughs.)
He never ate the tomatoes. *(She laughs again.)*
Uh
Well I had these lovely
little, orange
tomatoes that we had from the garden
and
and some homemade prosciutto
that was on the table
but they didn't eat that.
And he looked down the menu.
And he wanted the blackberry ice cream.
So we ultimately gave him that.
But it was a little bit of a dance,
I just kept bringing things
and when they ate it I would bring more
and just that kind of way.
I'm not even sure what all I brought him in the end.
I had thought
that I wanted to give him the "one peach dinner"
if he ever came to the restaurant.
I had sort of fantasized about that
'cause it's the most seductive
thing I could think of
and I would just give him peaches
in every form.
I would first,
you know I would give him sliced,
and then uh maybe in a little—,
Just a whole succession

of peaches.
So that he uh —
But a *great* peach.
The best.
Just picked.
That one.
and I, I
kept thinking he would really
he would understand something about peaches
and make transf——
ANNE DEAVERE SMITH V.O.: What about peaches?
ALICE WATERS: What about peaches?
Uh that when you eat a ripe one
when, when you have a food
that it's just
uh
ripe and delicious and or just made well
you know like a bread that
just a great bread that just came out of the wood oven
and you you you —
I think people are transformed by that kind of—
you know they, they have that experience and it's just
one of those unforgettable things in their lives
and I just thought
if I could give him
some thing
that he would be
um
you know Georgia peaches
it's a Southern thing
it's a food he's used to and maybe he hasn't had a great one
and that somehow I could reach him.

(She hands the peach to someone in the audience.)

Slide: Anonymous Man, Washington Insider

"Lambs to Dinner"

(In reality a white man in his forties, a Washington "Insider." He is wearing a tuxedo. There is a long table, as at a big black-tie dinner, with champagne glasses, ashtrays, half-eaten desserts, cups of coffee—the final course of a long evening. Candles are lit on the table.)

Now you're invited to the table in Washington
and everybody loves
"look at Anne (Heche)" and "look at Ellen (DeGeneres)."
And it's like these *lambs* are brought to the dinner and they're
    served up as *roast!**
I just thought the display was just so *off tune.*
Knowing Washington and
knowing how it would be perceived,
it was bowling alley.
It wasn't classy.
It was bowling alley.
It's been universally panned.
Gay you know
gay groups are pissed off that they were so
you know, laissez-faire in their sexual attitude in front of the
President.

---

*This refers to a White House Correspondents' Dinner that Ellen DeGeneres attended with Anne Heche.

Slide: Graydon Carter, Editor of Vanity Fair

"Well She Was Just Great"

(In reality an attractive, charismatic white man in his fifties. Downstage. Wearing a tuxedo, taking a French cigarette out of a container, lighting it.)

Well, she, she was just great, and, and so I invited her.
I mean not to be too
sort of cynical about this
but one of the things
you're supposed to sort of
uh
you're supposed to
you know,
you're supposed to try to bring an interesting guest
to the thing.
And um
so Ellen DeGeneres is um
so.
I, we asked her to this
and she said
yeah and I
thought Well shit
they're she
they're gonna make a big splash because
Washington is a very conservative place.

Slide: Graydon Carter, Editor of Vanity Fair

"Didn't Bother Me"

(Smoking a French cigarette, wearing a tuxedo.)

They were pawing each other a little too much at dinner for
    some
people
but uh
it didn't bother me.
Well,
they had their arms around each other the whole night
but it didn't bother me.
My staff thought it
might have
but it didn't at all.
Well, they thought,
"Oh my God
poor Graydon
you know
Ellen and Anne are literally *fucking* on the chairs
and, and right beside him in the dinner."
Basically I either didn't notice it that much
but it
it just didn't bother me.

Slide: Judith Butler, Scholar of Rhetoric/Author

"A Scream"

(In reality a white lesbian academic, a scholar of rhetoric at U.C. Berkeley. Downstage of the table. Wearing a leather jacket.)

It's a scream, I think it's all a scream.
I think really clearly
(Ellen and Anne) approaching the President with their arms
around each other
for the photo opportunity
in order to um to produce uh a sensationalist picture—
It doesn't strike me as
gay pride at its finest hour
if that's
what you're asking me. *(She laughs loudly.)*
For them to do that in that room
it's not as if they're, they're entering
sexuality into the scene.
Hardly.
Because where Bill Clinton is, there's already sexuality in the
    scene.
So in some ways, all they're doing is exposing the subtext of
    sexuality that's already in the room.
I mean he could never do that with his sexuality.
He would
it's totally,
totally, unacceptable.
Evidently she has more
power than he does. *(She laughs.)*

'Cuz she can do something
he cannot do and in doing it
she exposes the fact that
he can't do it.

Slide: Anonymous Man

"Way Too Academic"

(The same anonymous man as before. He is eating dessert robustly.)

Too Academic
way too academic.
Talking about something that Washington can't handle at all—
Sex.
And any kind of sex.
But like "*gay sex*"?
Like,
because you know
it's it's just not part of the *game*.
It's not part of what you *say*.
It's not part of—
It's a very tight WASP environment.
It's a very very enclosed
tubular environment.
You don't talk about depression.
You don't talk about foibles.
It's a town where you only talk about strength and
    manipulation,
and Machiavellian points of view.
So you don't let on weakness.
You know, if you say that you are,
have struggled
or are in *therapy*
with your wife

over your child's
drug addiction
you'd be . . .
You wouldn't be able to run for President
today if you were in *therapy*.
Sex is so *dangerous*.
Sex is so . . .
Look at the way people *dress* in Washington!
It's the most
sexless town!
Your your uh costume designer has to go, really, to *Pappagallo's*
you know.
It's the most unsexy place.
Look at the way people dress at those dinners!
You know
It's like they
they bought their stuff at
um
you know
at um
Loehmann's.

Slide: Graydon Carter, Editor of Vanity Fair

"That Arc"

(CARTER *lights another cigarette.*)

We went up to
I don't know somewhere in the Hilton
and so the door comes in *here,*
and there's all these people, clusters of journalists,
people getting awards and stuff
like that
and Ellen and Anne and George Clooney
and his girlfriend
and I are standing over *here.*
Well Clinton comes in and he just—
you can see it in his eyes.
His eyes
just work the whole room.
He just locks in
he knows where he's going.
And he can't make it too obvious
and come right here
cause that's
Ellen,
George Clooney the whole thing.
Okay.
He wants to get over here as fast as he can.
Well he's on *crutches.*
And so he starts off like this
and somebody said,
"Should we go over to him?"

I said, "I will put money
he will be here in front of us in five minutes!"
Sure enough,
hobbling along,
saying hello to here
saying hello to there
he just made
that arc so perfectly.
You know all these people are sort of cut out of
the thing
and boom—
He was there. *(Slight pause.)*
He looked great too.
(Slight pause.)
I've never been invited to the White House for dinner
and I wouldn't want to insult them,
but I probably wouldn't go.
I'd rather stay in the city with my kids.
I, I just probably wouldn't *go.*
Well, it's the most uptight place in the world!
I'm sure you can have a nice life there,
but I'd be just too terrified of,
if it's a-all built on power
uh
like
if I lost my job tomorrow, I'd be
I'd be *unhappy*
but I certainly
this is
you know
it wouldn't ruin my life.
But I think if you lost your big job in Washington,
it's over.
You gotta leave.

Slide: II. Sending the Canaries into the Mines

Slide: Anita Hill, Professor of Law

"Slick, Dirty"

(This section is set up with a long table that is bare. No covering. Metal. There are four table microphones set up, or one that can move up and down the table.)

(ANITA HILL *is a brown-skinned black woman in her forties.)*

First of all,
they used that whole idea of an uh
polygraph test as a threat.
They said, Well will you take a polygraph test, Ms. Hill?
So we called their bluff
then they accused us of inventing it as though
it was our idea to start with.
Then they said it's a trick.
It was slick, it was dirty.
And another thing that you might think about,
it was slick it was dirty,
but President Bush in many ways was protected from that dirt.

Slide: Maggie Williams, Former Chief of Staff to First Lady Hillary Rodham Clinton

"Lie Detecting"

(MAGGIE WILLIAMS *in reality is a brown-skinned black woman in her early forties.*)

I don't know if you've ever taken one.
Well,
you know,
it's like going to the electric chair.*
(*She laughs.*)
I mean
they strap you,
in
and put things all over you,
little wires that are connected to
your arms
like a blood pressure thing
and uh
I mean I kept thinking, you know the whole time,
when I was taking the lie detector test
and you sit in a chair and you think—
"Now what did I do in my life to get to the place
where I'm taking a lie detector test?"
Uh
ya know,

---

*She is referring to the Whitewater hearings, in which she had to testify.

I just
I just—
Ya know you just feel like a common criminal
(*She laughs.*)
is what you feel like,
is like a common criminal.

Slide: Alexis Herman, U.S. Secretary of Labor under President Clinton

"Washington Political Insider"

(ALEXIS HERMAN, *in reality, was a light-skinned black woman in her late forties, with a slight Southern accent.*)

There was a real possibility that I wouldn't have gotten through
you know,
you know,
the feeding frenzy.
And then the funniest thing to me was that
somehow I was labeled a "Washington Insider."
That was really, you know
that was really funny to me.
I've always felt
you know
as a black woman,
you know,
you're on the outside looking in,
trying to bring down the walls,
bring down the barriers
to be in the room
to get to the table,
you know?
You know.
My daddy was very active during his life,
You know,
he was the first black to sue the Democratic Party because they
wouldn't give him an

absentee ballot.
He just didn't take no for answers,
you know.
He wasn't a fiery man;
he was just steady and persistent,
you know?
But he had this quiet way of getting people out of trouble, you
    know,
in the South when they would get arrested or folk would end up
in jail in the middle of
the night or these —
we call it police brutality now;
I don't know what the name was for it then.
But people used to always knock on his door in the middle of
    the
night to say, So-and-so
has been put in jail;
can you come and get him out?
You know, he would show up in court sometimes to keep kids,
    you know, from being thrown in jail.
Their mamas were calling,
you know,
because during those days there wasn't any real justice, you
    know.
The courts were white people and all-white juries,
but yet he could go and talk to the judge and somehow get
    these
kids out of trouble.
So that was just how he was,
you know,
and they used to have these meetings,
the NAACP and a sort of group around Mobile,
he was a ward leader.

The only ward in Mobile where people could go and vote was
    Ward 10,
where my daddy was, like, the ward leader.
Anyway, I used to ride in the car with him at night.
You know, my parents weren't married.
My mom was a single mom,
but he was a very good father to me,
and he would come and pick me up from school,
you know,
and take me riding in the evenings.
And if he had his business to do,
you know, he would ride,
and I would go with him,
and I'd sit in those meetings,
you know,
and I'd sit over there with a coloring book or whatever;
but that's how he spent time with me.
So— and on Christmas Eve,
we always took these rides out,
you know,
and that's how he would put me to sleep and bring me back
    home.
So that's kind of what I did with him.
And this one Christmas Eve we were going over the bay to
    Father Warren, he's a
priest,
and—
I was only five.
And we went for our ride,
and he went to one of his meetings over the bay.
My daddy had a silver pistol with a pearl handle,
and he was a peaceful man.
I never heard my daddy curse or raise his voice a day in his life.

He kept his gun right here in the front of his old DeSoto.
Green and white.
We had lots of DeSotos
(but this one) was green and white.
But whenever there was *trouble,*
you know,
something was going *on,*
the gun came out from under here,
and he would always put it by his side.
Now, I used to like to sit up under my daddy when we would be riding,
and sometimes,
you know,
how daddies put you in their lap and let you steer the wheel?
But if the gun was on the *seat,*
then I knew that there was a problem.
He didn't tell me,
but that was the symbol,
and I would always hug the window,
you know.
I guess I was scared.
I was scared of that gun.
I wasn't necessarily scared of what was going on outside because
I didn't necessarily understand it contextually, but I was
scared of that gun,
you know.
(*Louder.*)
I didn't like that gun
because it was just a symbol of tension and something was
wrong,
and my daddy could be hurt.
You know, it was more of that.
I didn't want anybody messing with my daddy. So this particular

night the gun is out, we
go over the bay, we go over to Father Warren's,
and they were all in their meeting.
And we get back in the car.
In those days, over the bay, dark roads, dirt roads, no lights, the
    church is way back off the road.
And we're coming back from the meeting that night,
and, you know, the cars and the lights had come behind us, and
my daddy starts driving
fast, and we're trying to get around these cars, and they're,
you know,
pushing us off the side of the road with the cars, and he's hav-
    ing—
(Responding to a question.)
It's the Klan, yeah.
So we're kind of wobbling all round the trees and stuff.
So eventually he had to stop the car,
and he was perspiring.
My daddy, you know, he was real calm,
but he was perspiring.
So he just stopped the car.
He pulled over,
just stopped,
and he said,
you know,
he said,
"Poppy's got to get out of this car,"
and he says,
"I'm going to put this gun in your hand,
and I want you to get right down there,"
and he pointed, like, under the dashboard.
And he said,
"You get down there,

and Poppy's going to put this gun in your hand."
And he says,
"I'm going to have to get out of this car,
and I'm going to lock this door."
He said,
"If anybody opens that door,
I want you to pull that trigger."
And he took my finger and he put it right on that trigger and he
　　put that gun in my hand and I had it just like this and I was
　　down under the dashboard.
(*Responding to a question.*)
Oh, yeah. I was tiny.
I was only five.
I was always a small child.
And that's where I got.
I got down—on—the—floor—underneath—the—dashboard
　　by the seat
with the gun in my hand,
and he got out and locked the door,
and he just started walking to face the Klan.
And he told me,
Don't raise my head, don't look up, don't look out.
You know, I could hear 'em, you know.
I could hear 'em.
You know,
you could see the car lights and stuff, but mostly I could hear
　　'em.
What I remember more than anything were these sounds,
you know.
Yelling,
names,
and shouting.
I remember that more than anything.

That's why for years I didn't talk about this because I could hear
    those sounds.
"Nigger," you know,
"get him, kill him, beat him,"
you know, just, just sounds.
I just remember—I remember "*nigger*" more than anything.
    What I remember more than
anything was just the word "*nigger*";
"Get that nigger."
"Here comes that nigger,"
you know.
So, anyway, I just remember "*nigger*" more than anything.
So it seemed like forever.
I really don't know how long it was,
but it felt like forever that I was down there with this gun, and
eventually
I heard Father Warren's voice saying,
"Alexis, it's all right.
It's all right.
I'm coming to the car.
Don't do anything. Don't do anything.
It's Father Warren.
I'm coming to the car.
I'm coming to the car."
And, you know, he got to the car,
and he opened the door, and basically—
see, they knew that it was trouble that night,
you know,
that's what they had been meeting on.
So they had followed my daddy because they didn't trust him to
    get back to the city okay, like over the bay.
So they had a little posse that followed him, which they would
    do sometimes. But this night they had made a decision to
    follow Poppy, so they followed,

and luckily they did.
So they roughed him up,
you know,
by the time Father Warren had gotten there.
But they took him on to the hospital and somebody came and
drove me home.
Somebody drove me home. It might have been Father Warren.
    I don't remember.
They took my daddy wherever they took him because they had
    beat him up,
you know.
And then they took me home,
and I kind of remember seeing,
you know,
looking up,
and I saw them putting him in the other car;
Oh, his shirt was torn off.
I remember—
because my daddy was a neat man, too. That was the other
    thing,
and I think for a child's *impression*, to see my daddy's white shirt
torn off of him,
and he had straight black hair that he wore back,
and it was,
like, hanging all down around, you know.
And them carrying him.
I don't remember him being conscious.
And somehow to wear the *mantle* of a "Washington Political
    Insider"
was just funny to me
you know.
It was just funny to me.
ANNA DEAVERE SMITH V.O.: You grew up in the South with the
    Klan, and had some personal run-ins with them. We don't

have the Klan the way we did when you were a child. In a
word, what do we have now?
ALEXIS HERMAN: You say, In a word?
You know, unfortunately,
almost the absence of the *visible* and the *tangible*
leaves the impression
that the problem isn't *there*,
that the issues are not *there*,
you know. And so I think what you have
is this false sense,
really,
now, that everything is okay,
you know,
because you *don't* have the Klan.
So the flip side of that
is this immediate conclusion that it's no longer a problem,
    when it
still is.
And so I'm trying to figure how to say my feelings of it.
(*Pause.*)
Oh, I can't say that on tape.

"Making a Kind of a Political Point"

But the uh
the test itself was horrible
and I thought, once I had taken it,
"Well there
people will *have* to see
they'll *have* to see that
I'm telling the truth"
and then of course by the time I had taken the *second* one and passed it
I said, Well, you know, this is you know a hands-down situation.
Nothing changed according to the
questioning and the treatment,
in fact it got harsher.
What they care about is making a kind of a political point.
(Slight pause.)
And then they really didn't care about me.
I was just in the way.
I mean, I switched it from being so intent
on trying to remember things
and get ready
for these things
to just reading the Bible.
Because it was clear that they didn't care about anything that I had to say.
ANNA DEAVERE SMITH V.O.: Did you know that you were going to Washington to fight?

MAGGIE WILLIAMS: Oh no.
Oh no.
I wasn't going to Washington to fight.
I was going to Washington,
and I was going to work for the First Lady
because,
I had just, I mean,
my experience in having worked with her before,
was
you know we had worked on, I thought the most important
    issues
there were.
We worked on children and family issues.
And,
if she was going to keep doing that,
which I was sure that she was,
to me it seemed like
you know the most important thing I could do.
And she gave me such great hope,
quite frankly.
And that's what I thought I would be doing.
And
uhm,
I didn't think that I would
be having to
defend my
integrity?
And,
also the idea,
that you have people, chipping away,
at you know
this person that
you, and

your mother, and your father,
and all these other people have worked *so hard* to help
create—
And in an instant,
they can
uhm—
I didn't think
that I would be wasting so much
time.

Slide: Anita Hill, Professor of Law

"House Arrest"

I feel like I have,
a very limited space
and it's really limited to my physical home.
But
just the house,
just the house.
To some extent I'm more at home in Norman, Oklahoma, than
    I am anyplace.
It was just bizarre yesterday.
The first thing I did, I went to
a place to get a cup of coffee,
and the, the
woman behind the counter
said
"What—is—your—name?"
As though she was interrogating me!
As though I was some kind of an impostor.
She said
"Well I had heard that you hadn't lived in Norman in a long
    time."
And so,
you know what I *thought* was my home in some ways has been
taken away from me by these *myths* that go around.
So even in the town that I *thought* was my home
I can't go in and be completely anonymous,
and completely relaxed.
I still have to

deal with the question about who I am and what I'm doing
      here.
I think that (home) is as much psychological and spiritual as
      it is
physical.
To the extent that I am at peace here now
it's not because this place has fulfilled the promises we thought
      it
would it's because *I* have fulfilled the promises and faced up to
      its
limitations.

Slide: III. *Darkness at Noon*

Slide: Ed Bradley, 60 *Minutes Host*

"Captives"

(In this section, the characters simply change ties—that is, each character has a different tie—or if one actor, or fewer actors than characters, a change of tie signifies a change of character.)

(ED BRADLEY in reality is a well-dressed black man in his fifties.)

ED BRADLEY: *(Eating a carton of yogurt; shirt, tie, no jacket.)*
(The press and the President.)
Both are captives.
Um
I think the press is
individually and collectively a captive
of the White House,
(He puts a spoonful of yogurt in his mouth, and scrapes the cup.)
in that—
you go there every day—
and you stay there.
(He scrapes the yogurt cup.)
The press is ushered in
for
a specific period of time
a minute, two minutes
so they can get a picture,
they stand there with notes and pads,
eh

"Mr. President, what about Bosnia?"
Scream at him.
If he wants
if he has something he wants to say then he'll use that oppor-
tunity
he'll take advantage of it.
If he doesn't,
most of the time he'll ignore you.
Sometimes the President will say something
when he has no intention of saying something.
When it's not thought out,
and you get a free —
something.
But it's really a very limited exchange.
He's a captive —
because,
He's there.
Uhm —
It's a very
controlled existence.
Uh —
There's no freedom.
You can't just pick up and go.
You can walk out here today and decide —
"Well let me run over to Barney's I need to pick this thing up."
The President to do that has gotta take an entourage —
Somebody's gotta go there with dogs,
and uh eh
ya know it just becomes uh you you —
You are a *captive* of the White House.
True you have a lot of power, and there's a lot you can do with
it.
But you are a *captive*.

And the press
is very much a captive
because—
(Hits his hand on the desk along with the next line in rhythm.)
If he moves,
we move.
If he sits,
we sit.
(Hits the desk again.)
And people don't like to say it—
but everybody
particularly in those situations,
and given the climate and the world we live in today—
Everybody's on the death watch.

Slide: Christopher Hitchens, Journalist for The Nation *magazine,*
Vanity Fair

"Sex and Death"

(Drinking a Scotch, and smoking. HITCHENS *at table with food
that goes untouched. In reality* HITCHENS *is a white man in his
early fifties with a British accent. A sunny, nice restaurant in
Washington on a corner.)*

But what impressed me from the start was this:
it was (Clinton's) relationship between sex and death.
Death.
In the following way.
I went to New Hampshire
in Ninety-*two*
for *Harper's* magazine
Um
and it was the week
of the Flowers
flap.
And I must say from her tapes and her press conference,
however those were manipulated by the *Star* or the *Enquirer* or
whatever it was,
it was fairly obvious to me
that she had been telling the truth.
And probably had been in love with the guy
and that therefore it couldn't be
between them,
"Well she says that and I say the other thing."
He said

She said
never never actually really occurs.
Because if she's saying it and it's not true,
either I'm a liar
or she really is—
a menace.
She'd have to be
wicked.
So that means you'd have to trash her,
to impute a bad motive
you can't get out of it.
What would a woman have to do to make a thing up
like that?
A lot.
Clearly Flowers wasn't doing that.
Or so it seemed to me.
So that week,
Clinton was slipping in the polls
Clinton was expecting to win New Hampshire.
He actually never did.
He leaves the trail
goes back to Arkansas,
and supervises the execution of a mentally lobotomized
physically lobotomized,
There's a man called—
was a man called
Ricky Ray Rector
who had committed,
who had indeed committed uh murder.
He was already quite disturbed,
and having killed these people,
he put a gun to his own head and blew away his prefrontal lobe.
And he was *nursed* back to life

so that he could be executed.
Uh but he knew no more about what he'd done,
had no conception of it
and the best
the most encapsulating anecdote of this is that,
he was well known to be say, [*sic*]
when they brought him his tray every night,
his snack,
in jail,
he'd always leave his dessert on the side
of the tray and eat it later
save it.
And on the night they came
they read him his rights—
they came to say, "Well you've got to come now."
(they don't gas them in Arkansas, they use
lethal injections)
He said "Okay,
I'm ready,
but this is my pecan pie
I'm coming back for it."
And they realized then he didn't have any idea
what was happening to him.
So
I have heard, people in the Clinton camp be asked,
then and since,
"Just one question.
Would Mr. Rector be alive
if it wasn't for the New Hampshire primary?"
And say
"Well yeah he would be,
okay I admit it."
Well, I have no further questions.

Slide: Walter Shapiro, Columnist for USA Today

"Are You Now or Have You Ever Been?"

(In reality a white man, fairly conservative in his dress, big smile.)

(Change of tie, puts on glasses.)

And for the record I am keenly aware that I am being taped.
And not only I'm aware of it, but I enthusiastically accept.
And so, so
the day that Clinton first responded to the scandal
I guess it was a Wednesday
and I just remember just watching those interviews,
the Jim Lehrer interview and the Mara Liasson interview
and you know, just watching so closely with my colleagues
you know every
you know every single verb tense,
uh you know
for example
I think
in one of the
interviews
Clinton kept saying
"I am not having an affair with Monica Lewinsky"
or "I'm not having an affair"
which of course would lay open another double entendre
the issue had he had an affair?
It's why the nineteen fifties the red hunters kept saying, "Are
        you now or have you ever been a member of
the Communist party?"

(Pause.)
First of all,
of course I'm having a good time.
I mean there was a moment in December, January,
where I really was actively wondering whether I had made a
    totally
wrong career choice.
I mean here I am
growing up wanting to be a newspaper columnist,
and I really thought that how come all the good stuff, like the
    Cold War
Joseph McCarthy, Vietnam happened on Walter Lippmann's
    watch,
and I get Bill Clinton and the balanced budget?
Then suddenly we had *this*?
And *all* of life changed.
But, let's make no bones about it.
I mean
It doesn't get any better!
I mean this is life not only imitating art
It's doing *better* than art!

Slide: David Kendall, Attorney for President Clinton regarding Monica Lewinsky

"Is Is"

(Sitting at a table in white linens, opening his napkin, and beginning to eat soup. Jacket and tie, in reality a white well-heeled man in his forties or fifties.)

I thought that the actual, that
if you could ever get anybody back to what he was
saying,
they would understand that it was not so silly—to say
"It depends on what the meaning of *is* is."
He was retrospectively parsing what his lawyer was saying.
His lawyer—was, "There—is—no—sex,"
He said, "Look,"
And what he was asked,
"Wasn't your lawyer *wrong,*
and misleading the court?"
He said, "No,
It depends on what the meaning of *is* is."
What the President was saying was,
"When my lawyer said there is no sex he had been speaking of
        the *present.*"
That was an accurate,
that was an accurate
quote.
If however he meant there had never been *anything,*
putting aside the meaning of sex,
if there had never been anything *amorous* there

he would have been *wrong*.
Again,
the President is very <u>*smart*</u>,
He is *analytic*,
and he can
make distinctions which are very *fine*.
There's nothing wrong with that.
People have held up "Depends on what the meaning of *is* is"
as if it was perfectly self-evident, always, in all contexts
what the meaning of *is* is.

"Spinach Dip/Sad"

Coming back from Washington the night the Starr report came
    out, having gotten it from Kinko's copy shop.
It was kind of nice to just sort of be the center of attention at
    dinner with close friends and they would say something
and I would say, "Not exactly. Let me show you footnote four
    hundred thirty-two; the one about spinach dip."
But now,
that we're in for the long haul with this
the whole thing,
having now chortled about how wonderful it is,
The whole thing is sad.
The whole thing is sad.

Slide: Mike Isikoff, Investigative Reporter/Journalist for Newsweek

"Persistence"

(In reality ISIKOFF *is a white male in his forties. Columboesque. Wearing a trench coat and glasses.)*

You have to be persistent.
I mean
people hang up on you
people slam doors in your face.
One thing you do have to have that's important,
particularly on this stuff,
I don't know
you have to have a really thick skin.
(Responding to a question.)
Now you're putting me on the couch and I don't wanna go
    there.
I don't know.
But for this story, go back to *The War Room.*
It was the *shame* card that they use,
"Serious journalists don't ask questions about *stuff*
like this.
You're telling me you're a *tabloid* reporter?
You're asking me sleazy questions!"
Look at the way Mike McCurry describes me to Howie Kurtz in
    Spin Cycle!
"That *sleazy*," in the Kathleen Willey thing.
"This other new *sleazy* charge being promoted by another
    bimbo beat reporter Mike Isikoff
who goes around chasin' sex stories

how *cheap* and *tawdry*
scum."
They'll think you're *scum*.
They'll make fun of you.
You're a *bimbo* beat *tabloid* reporter.
That's the way they use this to keep people off of
this stuff. *(Pause.)*
There's a tawdry element to this stuff.
I just thought it was gonna be . . .
It was a story.
I thought that Clinton's private conduct was reckless,
and for the most part, most of these women were telling
the truth
and in that sense,
they were lying.
The Clinton people were lying, and the women were telling
    the truth.

Slide: Chris Vlasto, ABC News Investigative Reporter

"The—Blue—Dress"

(Wearing a black leather jacket, and no tie. In reality VLASTO *is a white male in his thirties, much more au courant than others in the play, big smile, eager to talk.)*

The—blue—dress.
Oh I knew about it the first day and nobody wanted to touch it before
before we broke it.
I had known that she,
I had heard that she had sent up a dress
that had semen on it
and
with all the gifts
to her mother in New York.
And I thought it should have been mentioned the very first day.
But
"Oh,
we can't bring that up!
Oh come on, Chris, shut up!
You cannot talk . . .
We don't want to talk about *semen*!
Oh no!"
And they're goin' on and on
"You can't talk about *semen*.
Go awaaay."

Slide: IV. Political Theater

Slide: The grand jury testimony of the forty-second President of the United States, William Jefferson Clinton, by the Office of Independent Counsel

(August 17, 1998.)

(A table is rolled out, and behind it sits the Representative of the Office of Independent Counsel. Shirt, white long sleeved, tie. No jacket. A microphone on the table, large stack of papers, a brief. From the actual grand jury testimony.)

OFFICE OF IND. COUNSEL: *(On a mike.)* If the person being deposed touched the genitalia of another person, would that be—and with the intent to arouse the sexual desire, arouse or gratify, as defined in definition (1), would that be, under your understanding then and now—sexual relations? Yes, it would? So, you didn't do any of those three things—including touching her breast, kissing her breast, or touching her genitalia?

Would you agree with me that the insertion of an object into the genitalia of another person with the desire to gratify sexually would fit within the definition used in the Jones case as sexual relations? I want to go over some questions again. I don't think you are going to answer them, sir. And so I don't need a lengthy response, just a yes or a no. And I understand the basis upon which you are not answering them, but I need to ask them for the record.

If Monica Lewinsky says that while you were in the Oval Office area you touched her breasts, would she be lying?

All I really need for you, Mr. President—

— is to say

— I won't answer under the previous grounds, or to answer the question, you see, because we only have four hours, and your answers—

— have been extremely lengthy.

The question is, if Monica Lewinsky says that while you were in the Oval Office area you touched her breasts, would she be lying?

If Monica Lewinsky says that you used a cigar as a sexual aid with her in the Oval Office area, would she be lying? Yes, no, or won't answer?

If Monica Lewinsky says that you had phone sex with her, would she be lying?

Let me define *phone sex* for purposes of my question . . .

Slide: United States President William Jefferson Clinton, President of the United States 1992–2000

Slide: From an interview conducted with the President by Anna Deavere Smith, October 29, 1997 (before the Monica Lewinsky scandal broke)

"Baby Huey"

(In the Oval Office, he wears a blue suit, a tie, and shoes.)

ANNA DEAVERE SMITH V.O.: Do you think you are treated like a
    common criminal?
CLINTON: I think
George Washington said that.
Well he said he was treated sort of like a common criminal.
I don't know about that.
No, I wouldn't say that.
But I think that in terms of the way,
uh, uh a President
in the White House
even far more than Congress gets pilloried in the press.
The political press has this image,
that the presidency is so all-powerful
that none of the presumptions
should apply.
No presumption of innocence.
No presumption that some techniques
and things are off
balance.
I think we really ought to ask ourselves,

Do we want to put our public officials in the position
of basically having to bankrupt themselves just to survive in
    office?
And I just think it's—gotten—out—of—whack.
I think that the thing is seriously—out—of—whack.
I was so naïve, that I really
believed them when they said,
if you were honest and forthright,
it would clear,
the air.
I mean it's *chilling* when you really think about what happened.
(Speaking very fast and emotionally.)
When Hillary's
legal
uh bills were found,
oh it was all over the papers right?
She had to go talk to a grand jury.
First Lady going to a grand jury.
Big pictures!
Now—
What happened?
We said,
We don't know where these came from but we're glad they
    turned up because they support *her*
story.
Why would we cover up records that support *her* story?
That was down in,
paragraph *ten* here.
Then what *happened*?
Another totally independent inquiry
by a Republican law firm
spent three point six million dollars
looking into all the documents

on the savings and loan
you know what it said?
"No basis for criminal action.
No basis for a civil suit.
The records
support Hillary's account!"
Did all those people
who *blared* the record discovery?
who *blared* the grand jury testimony?
all over America?
bother to tell the American people that
that's—what—this—
report—
done—by—a—Republican—law—firm
after they spent almost
four million dollars said?
No!
(Intense, raspy.)
Little bitty notice made!
(Leans forward.)
So
what I'm saying is—
Ya know, we're fine.
We're standing here.
We're showing up for work.
We're fine.
Bad for America.
Bad for the system.
Makes good people less willing to run.
And it corrupts the search for the truth.
Because,
the only target in town is the White House!
If Congress does this it's not so bad.

I told you what the Republican Senator told me—
He said
"Before you got elected we were stupid enough to think the
        press
was liberal
and then we realized."
He said, "Then you got more grief than anybody had ever gotten
before
and then we realized that they are liberal in the sense
that most of 'em vote Democratic.
They vote with you but they think like us."
And when I asked him what he meant he said,
"You're a Democrat.
You come here thinking you can do good.
You want to use the power of the government to make good
        things happen to improve people's
lives.
Republicans are *suspicious*
of the ability to make anybody's life better.
We like this because we have power,
and the press,
they want power.
So let 'em *vote* with you they think like us
When you're in
they get power
and *we* get power the same way.
We hurt *you*.
So never mind what the truth is,
hit the target.
Now
I just keep standin' up I'm like one of those old Baby Huey dolls
that we had when you're a kid.
You punch 'em and they come back up.

So I'm fine.
But it's bad for the country.
It's bad when the system doesn't care
whether the attack is true or not.
It's bad when the burden of proof is on the accused,
and you're supposed to disprove,
all conceivable accusations,
present,
and future,
and if you don't,
there's something wrong with you.
It's bad when innocent middle-class people who work at the
    White House
can be
bankrupted
by
exorbitant legal fees.
It's bad . . .

Slide: V. Moral Slippage

"Fat, Dumb, and Happy"

Slide: President George Herbert Bush

Slide: From an interview conducted with the President by Anna Deavere Smith, Washington, D.C., summer 1997

ANNA DEAVERE SMITH V.O.: We—probably don't think—I would
    say some behave as though maybe they don't think we need
    a President.

(He is drinking an Orange Crush and eating a chocolate chip cookie.)

As long as the economy is good, everybody is fat, dumb and
    happy,
that may be right.
We might not need a President.
The economy goes down,
people get thrown out of work,
that will change.
I hope that doesn't happen.
But when the economy is good,
we say, Hey, get the government out of my life.
I don't need it.
Who's the enemy anymore?
Why do we need foreign policy
or ambassadors or all of this,
and you have voices of isolation from the right

to some degree yelling "Come home America" kind of thing.
And joined by big labor
ah, "We don't want to export our jobs."
And so you have a kind of an interesting coalition.
But as long as the economy is strong and people are happy,
    overall, you're not going to have a great worrying, about the
    White House.

"Does a Tree Make a Sound?"

(In reality FLIP *was a white man in his forties.)*

(Speaking very fast.)

Norma McCorvey,
who's the Jane Roe of *Roe versus Wade*.
I can remember when I had the privilege of baptizing her,
I had the privilege of,
you know, leading her to Christ.
And what happened with Norma,
she's with us here,
and has been with us,
is here is Jane Roe of *Roe versus Wade*.
Sandra Cano,
of *Doe versus Bolton*,
those two cases which *legalized* abortion, number one.
And then made it—*Doe versus Bolton* made it legal through all
nine months.
Both of those ladies,
Sandra Cano and Norma McCorvey, neither one of them ever
        had
an abortion,
never, and, and they were used by the abortion industry,
they were *used* by the abortion industry to bring these class
        action suits.
Now both of them are confessing,
professing Christians that are doing everything they can to undo

the horror.
Well, what happened to them?
How did their politics change so much?
I mean, Jane Roe, let's face it,
was *the* spokesperson, the poster girl of the pro-choice
    movement.
But she jumped off the poster into the arms of Jesus!
What changes a person's politics is a change in the heart.
And that's what happened to me.
What changed *all* of my politics
and my whole worldview
was that some new King got in my heart,
and the same new King got into Ms. Norma's heart,
and Sandra Cano's heart,
and in people's hearts all over this country.
And that's what's happening!
Is the heart of the nation is changing,
but the laws are always lagging.
Laws always reflect the change in the heart.
ANNA DEAVERE SMITH V.O.: Do you think America has a soul?
FLIP BENHAM: There's no question but that we have a spirit,
because that is what caused us to be so united,
I mean, the Pilgrim forefathers that came over here.
Why was America reserved for the English?
Because they had the Bible!
Why not the French,
or at least the Spanish,
they had the Armada,
they were the great colonizers of the time,
not England!
But it was reserved for those people that had a *book!*
I mean, you look at this, and you find out,
what is the most quoted book of the founding fathers?

What book do they quote the most?

And their writings were voluminous.

And it's not like we, we hardly ever write.

It's the Bible.

You see, this is a forgotten book.

This is a book that nobody—I mean, it was forgotten by *me* for,
I didn't meet Jesus until I was twenty-seven years old, and I
thought this book was for people that needed a crutch.

As a matter of fact,

I thought Christians were people that committed intellectual
    suicide in kindergarten and didn't know any better.

But I found out

I just

my eyes were open,

and I was *stunned!*

I was,

I don't

I don't believe this yet!

And you see, what a psychiatrist couldn't do for me in a billion
    hours on his couch

spending bizillion of dollars for his counsel,

this book and this Jesus did in one divine moment in my life.

He turned my heart back toward home.

I was surrounded, north, south, east, and west by me.

It was *my* career, *my* life, *my* body, *my* rights, *my* choice!

Does that sound familiar?

"Not the church, not the state.

Women must decide their fate."

Why is it that the homosexual community is so busy being
around abortion mills?

What does the homosexual community care

about

reproductive freedom?

Well because they understand the battle
better than the church of the living God.
It's the same worldview.
Their worldview is my rights my body my choice.
And my one commandment is "Thou shall not get in my face."
Don't you judge me
Don't you dare judge me
Nobody can judge me.
I determine my own reality.
I think
therefore
I am—
René
Descartes
versus
the thing that says
I am
therefore
I think.
You know the whole answer of "Does a tree make a sound
if it falls in the middle of a forest and nobody is around
to see it,"
is really key and crucial to where you stand.
Are you at the seat of the serpent or at the seat of the
woman?
Then you look for the middle ground.
Can't we somehow find a middle ground here between the pro-
lifers
and those that believe in abortions?
The answer is, Of course, you can't.
There isn't one.
Well, the answer is that you're going to be one or the other.
The answer is you are either going to convert like I did, like Ms.
Norma did, or you're going to burn.

It's revival or death.

And that's the way it's always been, all through the history of the
Bible.

In this country, most clearly manifested in the mid-nineteenth
century over the issue of slavery.

In other words, you will resist the evil,

even if it means that you're going to be punished by your government.

Because the government isn't God, God is God.

Slide: Cheryl Mills, Deputy White House Counsel under President Clinton

"A Baby Face Down in the Water"

(In reality a black woman in her early forties.)

Well, see
I don't think the law is necessarily about rightness and wrong-
    ness.
I mean, I think that's a large part of what the law tries to capture.
Um, but it also tries to capture obligations and responsibilities,
or weed out obligations and responsibilities.
So, you know, it's that terrible paradigm of,
you see a baby face down in the water,
you don't turn it over,
did you commit murder?
No, our, our, our law says,
we're going to preserve that level of space for you and say, you
    have no, uh,
affirmative duty in this particular instance.
Um, even though it would have taken you *nothing*
and some states don't buy that,
and have passed Good Samaritan laws, and others haven't,
and they struggle with how to deal with that.
I think the law tries to do right and wrong,
but also tries to preserve and protect certain freedoms.

Slide: Paulette Jenkins, Inmate, Maryland Correctional Institute for Women

"Mirror to Her Mouth"

(In reality PAULETTE JENKINS *was a very beautiful black woman in her thirties wearing a simple, white T-shirt and jeans, no makeup, hair pulled back.)*

I began to learn how to cover it up
because I didn't want nobody to know that this was happening
    in
my home.
Ya know.
I wanted everyone to think that we were a normal family
and I mean
we had all the materialistic things.
But that didn't make my children pain any less.
I ran out of excuses about how we got black eyes
and busted lips and bruises
me and the kids.
I didn't have no more excuses.
But it didn't change the fact that it was a nightmare
for my children.
It was a nightmare.
And I failed them.
Dramatically.
Because I allowed it to continue on and on and on.
And that night that she got killed,
and the intensity just grew and grew and grew.
Until one night,
we came home,

from getting drugs,
and he got angry with Myeshia
and he started beating her.
And he just continued to beat her,
he had a belt, he would use a belt.
I'm just speaking of the particular night that she died.
And he beat her
and he put her in the bathtub.
And I was in the bedroom.
But before all this happened,
four months before she died,
I thought I could really fix this man
so I had a baby by him!
Insane?
Thinking that
if I give him his own kid
he'll leave mine alone.
And it didn't work.
We wound up with three children.
But the night that Myeshia died.
I stayed in the room with the baby.
And I heard him,
just beating her,
just beating her,
like I said he had her in the bathtub,
and every time he would hit her,
she would fall.
And she would hit her head on the tub.
I could hear it.
It happened continuously,
repeatedly.
(Whispering.)
And I dared not to move.
I didn't move.

I didn't even go see what was happening.
I just sat there and listened.
And then later
(*She sucks her teeth.*)
he sat her in the hallway
and
told her just set there
and she set there for 'bout
four to five hours
and then he told her to get up
(*Crying.*)
and when she got up she said she couldn't see.
(*Whispering, crying.*)
Her face was bruised.
And she had a black eye.
All around her head was just swollen.
Her head looked like it was two sizes of its own size.
I told him to let her go to sleep and he let her go to sleep.
(*Whispering.*)
The next morning she was dead.
He went in and checked on her for school.
And he got very excited.
And he said
"She won't breathe!"
I knew immediately that she was dead.
'Cause I went in
I didn't even want to accept the fact that she was dead.
So I went and took a mirror to her mouth.
There
was *no*-thing coming out of her mouth.
Nothing.
He said
"We cannot let nobody know about this,
so you got to help me."

And I agreed.
I agreed.
I didn't dare tell anyone.
'Cause I had been keeping it a secret
for years and years.
And it just seemed like secondhand to me
to keep a secret.
That night,
we went to the mall
and we told the police
that she had been missing.
We told like the security guards of the mall
that we had like *lost* her.
Ya know we fabricated this story and I went along with it.
And we told him that she had been missing.
But she wasn't missing.
So after that
we left the mall
and we told them what she had on
that night.
We got her dressed in the exact same thing
that we told the police that we had put on her.
And we got the baby
and we drove like out to
(*Hear her getting the slightest bit tired here.*)
I-95.
I was so petrified
and so numb
all I could look
was in the rearview mirror.
And he just laid her right on the shoulder of the highway.
My own chile.
I let that happen to.

Slide: Brian Palmer, Photographer/Journalist

"You're Here to Take the Picture"

(Putting his camera away in his camera bag.)

ANNA DEAVERE SMITH V.O.: Right. Would you—would you—did
    you ever think of a dilemma, the dilemma of being in this
    position where you could save the President's life or take
    the picture? Which one would you do?
BRIAN PALMER: If it came down to me,
I mean,
I would like to think that I would—
I mean,
I would obviously sort of make the choice to assist a human life.
A human, whether it's a—
I mean, it doesn't really
it wouldn't matter if it was the President.
I mean,
if it's someone getting beaten up in an alley
and there's something I can do about it,
I'm not going to stand there and take a picture of it.
I mean,
I've been in situations in New York,
in street situations
where I've perhaps, unwisely,
you know, intervened
and I've had my colleagues say,
"Yeah, you know,
you're here to take the picture.
You're not here to get involved."

I would like to think that
if I feel that it comes down
to a point where I can save,
you know, a person or keep a person from getting hurt unneces-
     sarily,
I would intervene.
I mean, if it's—
I mean,
in situations where you can't do anything,
like people with guns who are fighting each other—
I mean, if you step in between you get dead.
So, in those situations,
I would probably hang back and try to document
and then at least you would have that,
you know, sort of historical record of that event happening.
But I don't know. (Pause.)
I mean,
I'm always— I mean,
I've thought a lot, a lot, a lot about this.

Slide: VII. One Card at a Time

Slide: Blese Canty, Church Member

"Right by the Rope"

(In reality BLESE *was a black man in terrific physical shape, in his late seventies in the rural South. Wearing work pants and a work-shirt.)*

(Speaking slowly.)

Well
that was exciting day, [*sic*]
It was people from far off
and narrow.
They were here
because
it just coincident [*sic*]
that the President
of the United State [*sic*]
would come
to a little small town like
Greelyville.*
There's very few people know where
Greelyville at.
Very few people know where
Greelyville at.
And that why it was such
a exciting

*President Clinton went to visit Southern churches that were burned down in 1996.

that
the President to come here to
Greelyville.
A lot of people didn't believe
that it woulda never happened.
And some of 'em come just to
really see
is that the
President himself?
Or his
Vice President
or some of his workers?
But no this was the President
himself.
Well you know,
they had it barricaded off
and they had a rope around
so you couldn't get to him.
But otherwise we woulda
been about that far apart.
He wasn't way over yonder
and I way over here.
And I shake his hand.
He say "How you doin'?"
I say "I'm doin' fine."
I say "I'm happy for you
I glad I glad to see
glad for you to be here today
I'm glad to see you."
This is the first time I've seen a
President face to face.
I never have shake a President hand
never have look a President
in the eye in all my days.

Slide: Studs Terkel, Americanist Radio Host

"Communication"

(In a trench coat with a cane, wearing Hush Puppies, red socks.)

Moral Slippage that was a phrase coined by Jeb Magruder.
He was one of Nixon's boys.
Jeb Magruder was one of Nixon's boys and he went to jail.
If it goes along without being challenged.
You see?
It becomes big then.
Sometimes it's drop by drop and bit by bit and we accept it daily
now more and more.
A thoughtful citizenry is what it's all about.
Now things are getting rougher and rougher because of the
     technology.
So this goes to the old-fashioned phrase, it's hard, it's tough.
Grassroots.
See the cards are stacked.
Now how do you unstack this particular deck?
It's a hard job.
It's gotta be one card at a time.
Grassroots is an old-fashioned word
that did with personal contact
door to door
person to person.
So I can tell you of another funny
playlet.
The Atlanta airport is a modern airport.
And as you leave the gate,
there are these trains.

That take you to the
uh
concourse
and out to a destination.
You go on these trains
and they're smooth and
quiet and efficient and there's a voice you hear on the train.
The voice you know was a human voice.
See in the old days you had robots.
The robots imitated humans.
Now you have humans, imitating robots!
So you got this voice
on this train
"Concourse One
Dallas–
Fort Worth Concourse Two
Omaha
Lincoln."
Same voice.
Just!
as the train is about to go,
a young couple
rush in.
And they're just about to close pneumatic doors?
And that voice
without-losing-a-beat says
"Because of late entry we're delayed thirty seconds."
Just then,
everybody is looking at this couple
with hateful eyes
the couple is going like this shrinkin'.
And I
said "Oh My God!"
I'd happened to have had a few drinks,

before boarding
I do that
to steel my nerves.
And so
I
imitate a train call
holding my hand
over my —
"George Orwell,
your time has come!"
Everybody laughs when I say that
but not on that train!
Silence!
And they're lookin' at me.
And so suddenly I'm shrinkin'!
So there I am with the couple
the three of us
at the foot of Calvary
about to be *upped* you know.
Just then, I see a baby,
a little baby in the lap of a mother,
I know it's Hispanic 'cause she was speakin'
Spanish
to her companion
about a year old
a little baby with a round little face ya know
and so I'm going to talk to the baby.
So I say to the baby,
holding my hand over my mouth 'cause
my breath may be a hundred proof!
So I say to the baby
"Sir, or, madam . . .
what is your considered opinion
of the human species?"

And the baby looks
you know the way babies look at ya
clearly
and starts *laughing*
busting out with a crazy little laugh
and I say
"Thank God for
a human reaction!
We haven't lost yet!"
And so there we have it!
But the human touch!
That's *disappearing* you see.
So we talk about defin——
There ain't no defining moment,
for me!
All moments are defining and add up!
There's an accretion of movements that leads to where we are
     now,
in which trivia becomes news.
In which more and more, less and less, awareness
of pain of the other.
So this is an interesting dilemma with which we are faced.
I don't know if a used this or not,
I was quoting Wright Morris
this writer from Nebraska
"We're more and more into communications and less and less
into communication!"
So there you have it!
So okay kid!
I've got to scram.
I gotta go see my cardiologist!

End of Play

Piano

Production Credits

Piano was first produced as a workshop production in the Plays-in-Progress Program at the Amercian Conservatory Theater, San Francisco, March 9–18, 1988.

Its first professional production was at the Los Angeles Theater Center (William Bushnell, Artistic Director), spring 1990. It starred Pamela Gien and Madge Sinclair.

It was subsequently produced by the Institute on the Arts and Civic Dialogue, Harvard University (Anna Deavere Smith, Artistic Director), summer 2000.

Scene 1

(*1898. The house of a large sugarcane plantation outside Santiago de Cuba. The play is set in the sitting room of the house. It is a large room with a wood floor. Upstage, tall glass doors lead into the garden. Several pairs of French windows, left, look onto a forest area.*)

(*Stage right, large double doors open onto a hallway leading to the front door and the rest of the house. A baby grand piano stands near the French windows. There is a sitting area, right, with chairs and a few small tables. Occasionally birds indigenous to Cuba can be heard from outside.*)

(SUSANNA, *a tall woman of Congolese descent, wearing an intensely starched maid's uniform with long skirts, stands in the middle of the room. Her hair is thick and African but is forced back into a tight bun. She is talking to* SIDI, *also an African woman but of a different tribe with different features.* SIDI *has uncombed hair, is in ragged clothes and barefoot. An eight-year-old* GIRL, *her daughter [later named* ROSA], *stands next to her, holding on to her skirt. The* GIRL *is of mixed blood.*)

SUSANNA: The girl is too small. I cannot use the girl. She is a child.

SIDI: (*Spoken in a language that it is unlikely the audience will understand.*) She is a strong girl.

SUSANNA: I can barely understand what you are saying.

SIDI: She will work hard for you.

SUSANNA: *(Shakes her head.)* I haven't got all day. I don't understand your language.

SIDI: I cannot keep this criollito.

SUSANNA: I still don't understand.

(ALICIA, *a Castilian woman with porcelain white skin, enters carrying sheet music.)*

Señora. This woman wants to sell us this little girl.

(Pause.)

I think.

(Pause.)

I can barely understand what she is saying.

ALICIA: When you are finished, let me know. I want to play the piano.

SUSANNA: I could use someone to help me, but the child is so small.

ALICIA: She is too little to work. She is smaller than Carlito.

SIDI: We are starving. My husband ran away into the forest to fight the war. He was killed. We have no way. I told him not to go. I can't take care of this girl.

SUSANNA: You see what I am saying? It's impossible to understand her.

ALICIA: She is one of your people. Surely you can understand her, Susanna. I hope you have not forgotten your own language!

SUSANNA: Señora, Cuba has many Africans. I don't understand all their languages. I have enough to do to understand Spanish.

(SIDI *begins to walk away.*)

ALICIA: No! Don't leave!

(*Pause.*)

Tell her my husband is in Spain. Tell her that he'll be coming back. I can't pay for anything until then. Eduardo doesn't believe that we should buy people and neither do I. Those were the old days!

SUSANNA: This little girl will starve.

ALICIA: Eduardo says that it's wrong to buy people.

SUSANNA: This is different. Eduardo's ideas are not so realistic.

ALICIA: Susanna, you don't believe in buying people either.

SUSANNA: I believe in many different things. Eduardo is not here. This is his idea that we should pay money for help, and that we should not buy people from others. But if he doesn't leave any money what should we do? I could use the girl.

ALICIA: We will take your girl. We will feed her in exchange for work.

(SIDI still has her hand extended.)

SUSANNA: Señora, she wants something in exchange for the girl. You cannot have the girl for free.

ALICIA: But it's not for free. We will feed her, she can live here. . . .

SUSANNA: You need to give her something in exchange.

ALICIA: Perhaps a pig? Or a lamb? Some flour? What do you think, Susanna?

SUSANNA: Come with me. We will give you one pig for the girl.

(SUSANNA briskly turns, indicating to SIDI and the GIRL to follow. They exit. ALICIA sits at the piano and spreads out her music. She plays the first forty seconds of Edward MacDowell's First Modern Suite, opus 10, first movement.)

(Off.) It is getting better, Señora!

ALICIA: *(Yelling off to SUSANNA.)* It is so exciting!! These wild American composers! They will make cuckold of my Brahms! *(She giggles.)*

Scene 2

(6:00 A.M. EDUARDO, *a handsome Castilian man, is seated near the windows, fully dressed.* SUSANNA *enters with the* GIRL. SUSANNA *carries a bucket and brush. The* GIRL *holds on to* SUSANNA'S *skirt.* EDUARDO *looks up.* SUSANNA *has a stick, like a long baton—about four feet long.*)

SUSANNA: I am sorry, señor. . . . Did you want your breakfast in here? It is not ready yet, but if you wish, I could tell them. . . . I did not mean to disturb you. I want to show the girl how to wash the floor.

(EDUARDO *rises, without looking at the* GIRL, *and exits.* SUSANNA *quickly walks to the upstage right corner of the room, her skirts flowing.*)

Every time you wash the floor, you begin here. Watch. (*She gets down on her hands and knees and scrubs with the brush.*) Try.

(*The* GIRL *does not move.*)

Come!

(SUSANNA *hits her thigh and the* GIRL *immediately comes to her knees next to* SUSANNA.)

Good! Take the brush! Take the brush!

(SUSANNA *grabs the* GIRL's *hand and puts it on the brush. She moves the* GIRL's *hand back and forth. She takes her own hand away. The* GIRL *stops.)*

No! Don't stop. Go! Go! More! More! *(She pushes the* GIRL's *hand again, then takes her own hand away.)* Good.

*(*SUSANNA *rises; the* GIRL *immediately rises too.* SUSANNA *goes toward the corner upstage left.)*

(The GIRL *follows, holding* SUSANNA's *skirt.)*

(She walks on; the GIRL *follows close behind.)*

*(*SUSANNA, *recoiling, stands absolutely still. The* GIRL *suddenly moves two feet back, scrambling backward.* SUSANNA *walks on.)*

Then you wash all of this. Then you come to this corner here. Then you come down further all the way down here, by the window, and all the way here to the porch.

(Mumbling.) Everyone is going to work. The bells are late. But you and I were not. We started on time! Who is ringing the bell so late? Stupids! Waiting for the bells. It's as if the whole world was a great big church. *(She beings to scrub again, moving toward stage right.)*

(The GIRL *stays under the bench. In exasperation,* SUSANNA *throws her arm up and lets it land on the side of her thigh, in a gesture of giving up. The* GIRL *comes out from under the bench, moves to* SUSANNA. SUSANNA *points with her baton to under the piano.)*

Always come to the piano this way from the side. From the side beside the window. Never come to the piano under the bench. Okay? If you come to the piano under the bench, the pedals will push your fingers into the floor, holding them like a crab. Okay? When you wash the floor under the piano, never touch the brush on the feet of the piano. You see these yellow lion's feet? Do not touch them.

(The GIRL *goes to take the brush. The* GIRL *begins to scrub.* SUSANNA *comes out from under the piano.)*

Careful. Careful. Stop! Stop!! *(She stamps her foot.)* Do — not — touch — the — feet! They will *eat* you!

(The GIRL *begins to scrub.* SUSANNA *keeps the brush away from the feet by guiding it with the baton.)*

Good. Come! Come! Bring the bucket. Bring!

(The GIRL *tries to stand.)*

No! Mother Maria, do I have to call for Chango to make you understand?

*(*SUSANNA *goes to the bench. She bangs her thigh. The* GIRL *follows.)*

Never touch the bench. Never. Never touch the red cloth over the keys. Never. *(She pauses, then swiftly lifts the red cloth from the keys.)* And if the red cloth is not over the keys, do not touch the keys. The keys are the teeth of the lion. They will chew you up and spit you out.

(The GIRL *mimics her, the pace and rhythm of her movement exactly the same.)*

Now watch. (*She touches middle C. It sounds.*) Bad! No! No!
Never do it! Never do it! Try. Try!

(*The* GIRL *touches middle C. It sounds.*)

No! No! Never! Bad! (*She slaps the* GIRL's *hand two or three
times. The piano sounds with every slap as the* GIRL's *hand is
still resting on the keys.*) Again! Again!

(*The* GIRL *moves her hand to the keys and hesitates.*)

Good! That's all! That's perfect. You are smart! You are
smart like a Spanish. Now. Let's go. (*She stands in the middle of the room, pointing with the baton.*) When you have
scrubbed under the piano, you will come to the middle of
the floor, which is very easy.

(SUSANNA *points to the middle of the floor with the baton. The*
GIRL *is still staring at the keys.*)

(SUSANNA *goes over to grab the* GIRL. *The* GIRL *jumps.*)

Oh. I forgot to put the red cloth over the keys. (*She whisks
the cloth over the keys and then sails past the* GIRL.)

(*She snaps her fingers in the air. The* GIRL *follows her. She points
to the brush and the bucket. The* GIRL *falls to her knees immediately and scrubs the middle of the floor.*)

(SUSANNA *stamps her foot. The* GIRL *leaps to her feet, scrambling
and stepping into* SUSANNA's *skirts.* SUSANNA *quickly pulls her skirt
away from the* GIRL's *feet.*)

Let's go. Bring the bucket. Bring!

(The GIRL *scrambles to lift the bucket.* SUSANNA *turns and moves toward the hallway. Her skirts sail, and she snaps her fingers behind her at thigh height like the conductor of an orchestra or a maître d'.)*

Scene 3

(The GIRL *is scrubbing the floor.* ALICIA *and* MARTINE *are at the piano. The* GIRL *stops scrubbing.)*

*(*ALICIA *sits at the piano, taking the red velvet cloth from the keys. The* GIRL *does not move.)*

*(*ALICIA *begins to play the MacDowell* First Modern Suite, *first movement.)*

MARTINE: No. It's very different, very different. It's not like Brahms, Beethoven, anyone else we have been studying. Watch.

(She rises, he plays. The GIRL *is stunned. She freezes until* ALICIA *gives her another glance. She scrubs the floor.)*

ALICIA: But let me try.

MARTINE: But of course.

ALICIA: MacDowell! What a composer! Why not invite him to Cuba?

MARTINE: No.

ALICIA: Why not?

MARTINE: Not until you can play the song better.

*(*CHAN *enters.)*

ALICIA: Oh. Chan! I didn't see you.

CHAN: You have a guest for lunch today, Señora. Have you forgotten?

ALICIA: A guest?

CHAN: The American journalist?

ALICIA: Oh! Well. That's fine. Did you remind Eduardo?

CHAN: Eduardo is bathing.

ALICIA: What time is it?

CHAN: Lunchtime.

ALICIA: Why didn't the bells ring?

CHAN: Emiliano, who rings the bells, has disappeared.

ALICIA: Disappeared?

(*Pause.*)

Well then someone else must ring the bells. We all need to
know when it's lunchtime, when it's time to wake up, and so
forth. We can't just do things at any time we like. Give our
guest something to drink, and I'll be back.

(MARTINE *catches the* GIRL's *eye.*)

Scene 4

(The GIRL is scrubbing. ALICIA is playing the piano. She is struggling with the Andantino and Allegretto of MacDowell's First Modern Suite. She is extremely concentrated. EDUARDO is at the window reading a letter. MARTINE is sitting near ALICIA at the piano. CARLITO, the son of ALICIA and EDUARDO, eight or nine years old, enters with SUSANNA and a cello. He looks like a little man, dressed in a suit with a vest and tie. His clothing is as stiff as SUSANNA's. He stares at the GIRL. After a moment, EDUARDO looks up.)

EDUARDO: Carlito, don't stare.

ALICIA: *(Stops playing.)* Carlito. Come. *(Pause.)* Come.

SUSANNA: Señora. Before you begin. May I please ask about Señora Theodora?

ALICIA: Yes.

SUSANNA: Shall we put her in the room over the pond, or shall we put her in the room facing the west hills? In the past she has stayed in both.

ALICIA: Put her in the room facing the west hills.

EDUARDO: When does Teddy arrive?

SUSANNA: Tomorrow, Señor.

CARLITO: *(Screaming.)* Teddy is coming tomorrow?

SUSANNA: Carlito, haven't we talked about how important it is to speak softly?

(SUSANNA *exits.*)

CARLITO: I thought Teddy was coming next week.

ALICIA: Weren't you counting the days?

EDUARDO: Ah! So you lost count! Let's hope you can keep your count in your music lesson.

CARLITO: (*Screaming.*) I love Teddy!!!!!

EDUARDO: Carlito, you are getting too old to scream and yell. If you scream and yell you'll have to work with the horses and the bulls all your life, and you are not cut out for that.

(CARLITO *goes to his mother. He holds his cello correctly, preparing to play, as* ALICIA *shifts her music.* SUSANNA *exits.*)

Where is your music, Carlito?

MARTINE: It is in his heart and soul. He knows it.

EDUARDO: Impossible.

ALICIA: Sssh. We are about to begin.

(ALICIA *starts to play Schumann's* Carnavale, *opus 9.*)

EDUARDO: He is making mistakes.

MARTINE: Give him a chance. The cello is very difficult.

ALICIA: Ssssh. All of you. You're like maiden aunts!

(CARLITO *and* ALICIA *continue to play. The* GIRL *is scrubbing.* CARLITO *watches her as he plays.*)

EDUARDO: Carlito is making mistakes because he is busy watching the girl! Carlito, don't stare.

ALICIA: Eduardo, if you must speak while we are doing our music lesson, then you can go into the garden and talk to yourself.

(CHAN *enters. He is quiet until they finish.*)

ALICIA: That was very difficult. Really, Eduardo, you make us nervous. And you talk talk talk talk talk. We don't play music while you're talking, why must you talk while we play music?

MARTINE: But may I make a suggestion? This part right here, if you do it like this, it will be easier for Carlito to follow. Watch.

(MARTINE *plays for just a few seconds.*)

CHAN: Excuse me, Señora.

ALICIA: Yes, Chan.

CHAN: The American journalist is here.

ALICIA: Henry?

EDUARDO: Again? I'll go and see what he wants.

(He rises. CARLITO *is staring at the* GIRL, *who is scrubbing. As he exits, he says:)*

Carlito, I told you to stop staring.

*(*MARTINE *is playing something over and over again on the piano, [Schumann's* Carnavale, *opus 9].)*

MARTINE: Carlito, try it with me. Try.

*(*CARLITO *tries.)*

*(*CHAN *enters.)*

MARTINE: It's much, much easier for him, if you do this allegretto. See.

*(*ALICIA *sits on the bench beside him.* HENRY *enters with* SUSANNA. ALICIA *gasps.)*

ALICIA: Henry!

HENRY: Oh, I'm sorry, I didn't mean to shock you.

ALICIA: Didn't Eduardo come out to meet you?

MARTINE: Most probably Eduardo is in the west hallway.

HENRY: I'm afraid I wandered a little. It's such a beautiful house. Could you tell me a little about your paintings? There are so many of them. And a few of the European masters, I think.

ALICIA: I'm in the middle of my music lesson.

HENRY: I was just writing a little something for the paper, about the houses here in Cuba. You have quite a collection of paintings. A veritable gallery!

ALICIA: What paper would this be?

MARTINE: He writes for the *New York Tribune*.

SUSANNA: I asked him, Señora, not to touch the paintings.

HENRY: Oh, I wasn't actually touching them, I was just, well, I was admiring the frame of one of them.

ALICIA: I'm happy of course to talk with you about the paintings. My family collected art for quite some time. So it would be an extensive discussion.

HENRY: Oh. Right. It's just that I need to send my editor the story right away.

MARTINE: And we are in the middle of our music lesson.

ALICIA: Was there a particular painting? You are curious about?

SUSANNA: It is Velázquez, Señora. The one with the Last Supper of Christ in the shadows.

(She exits.)

MARTINE: That's a complicated painting.

ALICIA: I simply can't talk about the paintings right now.

HENRY: How about Eduardo?

MARTINE: He knows nothing about paintings. He can tell you about horses, sugar, Negroes, Indians, wines, rum, women, but he can't talk about paintings.

HENRY: Shucks.

ALICIA: Come back tomorrow. I have a friend coming. I went to college with her. Smith College.

MARTINE: A coincidence.

ALICIA: We'll roast a big pig.

HENRY: Thank you for the invitation.

(EDUARDO *enters.*)

EDUARDO: Oh, there you are!

HENRY: It seems that I was in the east hall. And you were in the west hall.

CHAN: We don't have any pigs ready to roast, Señora.

ALICIA: Nothing ready to be killed?

CHAN: Nothing ready to be killed at this time.

ALICIA: How about a lamb!

CHAN: A lamb is possible.

CARLITO: *(Loudly.)* Oh no! Not a lamb!

EDUARDO: Carlito. What have we been saying about how loudly you speak?

CARLITO: *(Softer.)* Oh no, not a lamb.

ALICIA: Don't worry, it's not your lamb. In fact, you can go with Chan and pick the lamb, to make sure it's not your lamb. Okay?

Scene 5

(ALICIA is inspecting flowers in a vase. SUSANNA is with the GIRL. She now carries a stick longer than the baton she used in Scene 2. The GIRL comes with the brush and gets on her knees with her buttocks toward SUSANNA, who is holding the stick.)

SUSANNA: Now you are smart enough to get closer to the lion's feet without touching them. That is the only way to get the floor very clean. Take the brush closer to the lion. Do not hurt him. Good, good. Closer. Get the dirt from the lion, but do not hurt him.

(The GIRL stops suddenly.)

Do not stop.

(The GIRL takes her skirt and, getting close to the feet and putting the brush aside, wipes the floor with the skirt.)

Good!!! You are smart! You are smart like a Spanish! You are very, very smart. Come! Come here! To Susanna! Come!

(The GIRL cautiously comes out from under the piano.)

Now. I am going to give you this rag. Because you are very, very smart. But you see, yes? Only—use—the—rag—to—wash—between—the—lion's—toes. But. Never—hurt—the—lion!

ALICIA: What is the matter with Han? These flowers are wilting.

CARLITO: Mami!

ALICIA: Just one second, Carlito.

CARLITO: Teddy is here!!!!

(SUSANNA *exits.*)

(CARLITO *runs out of the room and comes in pulling* TEDDY, *an attractive American woman.*)

TEDDY: Alicia!

ALICIA: Teddy! You—look—great!!!! Look at your clothes!

TEDDY: I brought you some.

(*They embrace, laugh, et cetera.*)

ALICIA: Teddy!!

TEDDY: Alicia!

ALICIA: But look at this fabric. Is it French?

TEDDY: American.

ALICIA: The colors.

TEDDY: You don't think it's too bright?

ALICIA: I love it.

(HAN *enters.*)

TEDDY: Han! Hello! It's been so long!

HAN: Welcome to this house, Señora.

(SUSANNA *enters.*)

SUSANNA: Let Han know if there's anything you need. Rosa! Come! Come!

(SUSANNA *exits as* CHAN *enters.*)

CHAN: There's a man outside, Señora. He says he's with you.

TEDDY: He is.

ALICIA: You didn't tell me you were bringing a guest.

TEDDY: Didn't you get my letter?

ALICIA: We have trouble getting letters sometimes.

TEDDY: I hope it's not an imposition.

ALICIA: Don't be loco. You're my sister! This is your house, too! Chan, is something wrong?

CHAN: No, not at all. I just wanted Señora to know that the men from the stables wanted to greet her, but there are fires in the hills and they are fighting them.

ALICIA: Now, Chan, must you greet our guest with bad news?

TEDDY: That's not bad news! I mean, it's my house, too, right? We're family. So if it's your news, it's my news.

Scene 6

(*Evening.* MARTINE, HENRY, TEDDY, EDUARDO, ALICIA *are having drinks.* CHAN, SUSANNA, HAN, ROSA *are serving. They are a very attentive staff, the kind who never miss a beat. They watch everything very closely. If something needs to be refilled, et cetera, they do it immediately, taking their cues from the glances of* SUSANNA, *who silently runs the room.* CARLITO *is attentive to the conversation. His cello is in the room.*)

(*Ad lib* ALL *talking at once.* ALICIA *laughing.*)

HENRY: Teddy here agrees with everything I'm saying. Don't you, Teddy?

TEDDY: What's that supposed to mean?

HENRY: Your father owns land here.

TEDDY: How did you know that?

HENRY: Everybody knows that.

TEDDY: Who's everybody?

(ALICIA *laughs loudly.*)

HENRY: Your father's land isn't going to be worth very much. Soon.

EDUARDO: You're wrong!

HENRY: What's this we hear about cruelty?

(Long pause.)

That the Spaniards are doing repeated acts of cruelty to the natives.

(EDUARDO guffaws.)

ALICIA: Prop-o-ganda!

EDUARDO: Is that what they are saying?

ALICIA: Prop-o-ganda! I went to school in America. I know America. The disparity between what I would see in American newspapers and what I knew was going on at home was as wide as the full length of keys on the piano.

(SUSANNA exits.)

EDUARDO: You call yourself a journalist? To me it sounds like you're writing a novel!

HENRY: I don't write for the funny papers. I'm a serious journalist.

ALICIA: What are those? Funny papers.

TEDDY: They're new. We didn't have them when we were in school. They're cartoons. In our newspapers. And they have colored ink. Yellow ink. They're very influential these days. The funny papers.

(MONROE enters.)

ALICIA: Ah, Monroe! Henry, this is Monroe. He is traveling with Teddy.

(MONROE *sits. Long pause.*)

(MONROE *gives* TEDDY *a box of Cracker Jacks.*)

TEDDY: We have a surprise for you, Carlito!!!!! From America! It's a brand-new thing.

EDUARDO: It's okay to open it, Carlito.

(CARLITO *opens the box.*)

TEDDY: Try them.

HENRY: Cracker Jacks. It's a new product. People are crazy for them. I'd love to try them myself. They became popular since I've been stationed here.

EDUARDO: It's all right to try them, Carlito.

ALICIA: Let's all try them!

(SUSANNA *glances at* CHAN. CHAN *goes with an empty bowl on the tray and takes the Cracker Jacks, pours them in the bowl, and gives them to* HAN, *who begins to serve them.*)

ALICIA: How strange! But wonderful! Cracker Jacks!

(HAN *offers some to* MARTINE, *who shakes his head no.*)

ALICIA: Oh, Martine! Don't be so stiff! Try them! I love America because it's fun!

(TEDDY *goes to* CHAN *and whispers something to him.* CHAN *nods, and leaves.*)

HENRY: I don't know how much fun America is going to seem to be to you a year from now.

EDUARDO: Here you go again. Politics, politics, politics.

TEDDY: So, Henry, what's your plan?

HENRY: I'm just . . . around.

TEDDY: Are you going to be writing a story about my friends?

HENRY: Well. Maybe.

TEDDY: Alicia, do you want to be in the American newspapers?

ALICIA: It might be fun.

TEDDY: My father learned how to stay out of the American newspapers. And I think Cuba ought to be careful.

EDUARDO: Cuba is one thing, your father is another. Your father is a man. Cuba is a country! Why would Cuba be afraid of the newspapers?

(CHAN *brings* TEDDY *a cigarette, which he lights for her.*)

ALICIA: Teddy and I have known each other since we were four years old. She came here to play, I went to America to study. Supposedly. But I left all the studying to Teddy.

TEDDY: That's not true. You studied too. Philosophy as a matter of fact. And mathematics.

EDUARDO: It's true, Alicia studied mathematics, but to look at my books after she goes shopping, you would think that all she learned was division and subtraction, and missed school on the days they studied multiplication and addition.

Carlito, that's enough of those . . .

HENRY: Cracker Jacks.

(CARLITO *is about to put one more in his mouth.*)

EDUARDO: No more. Carlito. I said. No. More.

CARLITO: I was just trying to give one to . . . ? (*Referring to the* GIRL.)

EDUARDO: I said. No. More. Of any kind. For any reason. We've had enough of those Cracker Jacks!

(*Pause.*)

ALICIA: You can have some tomorrow, eh, Carlito? Han. Take these, and save them so that Carlito can have them tomorrow.

(SUSANNA *takes the Cracker Jacks from* HAN *and exits.*)

(*Beat.*)

ALICIA: Monroe, is there something you need?

MONROE: I wanted to look at Carlito's cello.

ALICIA: Go right ahead!

HENRY: Weren't you supposed to marry the cousin of Hamilton Fish? I can't think of his name, what's his name . . . ?

TEDDY: Is that what you heard?

HENRY: So, is Monroe the reason your engagement fell through?

TEDDY: *(Sharply.)* Excuse me?

HENRY: *(As if he had touched a hot stove.)* Just asking.

ALICIA: I don't see any problem if Monroe *had* been the reason
for the engagement falling through.

TEDDY: Alicia!

ALICIA: Here in Cuba we are all mixed up! I may be part African
for all I know. Our history is deep and complicated.

EDUARDO: I can assure you, Alicia is not African. This is a fantasy
of hers.

ALICIA: At any rate. Monroe is welcome in this house.

HENRY: I never suggested he shouldn't be!

TEDDY: Are you looking for a scandal, Henry?

HENRY: No need to get heated. I got a wrong lead here from
Eduardo, who says Monroe was your "beau."

ALICIA: 'Duardo!!

EDUARDO: I'm sorry. Teddy, you have been known to do things that are out of the ordinary.

HENRY: Is he your servant?

TEDDY: That's it! I'm done! Alicia, I had no idea that we would be dining with a scandalmonger. *(She rises to leave.)*

HENRY: What's the matter if I call someone a servant? It's good work!

ALICIA: This is a party! Let's not get so serious! Teddy, sit! Sit!

MONROE: Where'd you get this cello?

ALICIA: From my grandfather.

MONROE: I thought so.

(Pause.)

Must have been made . . . would you say it was made before . . . 1783?

MARTINE: Finished in December of seventeen eighty-two to be exact.

MONROE: I could tell.

MARTINE: Do you play the cello?

MONROE: I like to look at them.

(He stands and replaces the cello, then sits.)

(*Pause.*)

ALICIA: All right! Concert! It's time for a concert! Martine. Please, take your place at the piano. Martine and I have the pleasure of presenting to you a beautiful song, that I will sing, to his accompaniment.

(ALICIA *sings.* MARTINE *accompanies her. [Schubert's "Ungeduld" from Die schöne Müllerin].*)

(EDUARDO *applauds heartily.*)

EDUARDO: That is a beautiful song, sung so well by my beautiful wife! Every time she sings that song, I fall in love with her all over again!

(EDUARDO *goes to* ALICIA *and displays some sort of affection.*)

(CARLITO *goes to* HAN *and stands next to her, patiently waiting to be acknowledged for a request. She ignores him.*)

TEDDY: Henry, if my visit here or anything about me ends up on the society pages, I know a lot of people who can get you fired.

(HENRY *guffaws.*)

HENRY: I presume your visit has to do with your father's plantations.

TEDDY: That's none of your business.

HENRY: I heard your father was very ill.

TEDDY: That's none of your business.

HENRY: Isn't he recuperating now at your summer house out west?

TEDDY: We don't have a summer house out west.

(SUSANNA *enters*.)

HENRY: I'm sorry. I mean your ranch. Hey, didn't I read somewhere that they were using your father's ranch to train Rough Riders?

TEDDY: That's none of your business, either.

MARTINE: The Rough Riders are boys with cows, no?

HENRY: Cowboys. A lot of them are cowboys.

ALICIA: All those trips to America, all those holidays I spent on your ranch, Teddy, and you never once introduced me to a cowboy. It's not fair. Whenever you were in Cuba we introduced you to everyone there was to meet.

(CARLITO *is still standing next to* HAN.)

EDUARDO: (*Impatient*.) Carlito, what is it? Why are you standing there next to Han?

CARLITO: I wanted to know if the girl could have some.

EDUARDO: What girl?

(CARLITO *points to* ROSA.)

MONROE: That pretty little girl standing in the corner.

ALICIA: What is it that you want the girl to have, Carlito?

HAN: He wants to know if she can have some . . . Cracker Jacks.

HENRY: Hey! Good pronunciation!

EDUARDO: But I told you to take the . . .

HENRY: Cracker Jacks.

EDUARDO: *(With more violent rage than the moment would seem to warrant to* HAN.*)* I told you to take them away!

(Pause.)

SUSANNA: Señora, I do not think it's appropriate. For Carlito to feed the girl. Perhaps, if you don't mind, I will take Carlito in to have his dinner?

(Beat.)

ALICIA: Yes, yes. It's getting late.

*(*CARLITO *and* SUSANNA *exit.)*

(Pause.)

MONROE: It must have been difficult to get a piano here. To Santiago. Across the ocean. Up the hills! A lot of work! Yes?

ALICIA: It was! Very difficult.

MONROE: It must be difficult to keep it in good condition. It's so humid here! And the dirt from the hills?

ALICIA: It is difficult. Yes. Very difficult. Very difficult.

MONROE: It's a beautiful piano.

ALICIA: Thank you. *(Pause.)* Thank you. Martine! Play us something sweet and playful! And no love songs! Even they seem to lead to arguments.

(MARTINE *plays. [Scarlatti Sonata, D minor K.1].)*

Scene 7

(One month later.)

(The GIRL *jumps. Throughout the following scene between* SUSANNA *and* ALICIA, *the* GIRL *will stand still with the rag hanging from her hand.)*

ALICIA: She is so high-strung. She thinks I am going to play the piano. Look, how she smiles. But, today, I am not going to play the piano. Susanna, Eduardo's brother is coming from Spain. We have to talk to the cook. Will you come with me?

SUSANNA: We will make ochinchin every night. I remember, he is a wonderful man. He loved ochinchin. He wanted to take me to Spain, me and the cook.

ALICIA: No. No. Not that brother. Antonio. I am talking about Antonio. The general.

SUSANNA: Oh.

ALICIA: You see? We will only make Spanish food. That is all he ever eats. Even when he is in Paris.

SUSANNA: I think I remember him.

ALICIA: You have never met him.

SUSANNA: No? Not even when Carlito was a baby? Not even when we went to Madrid?

ALICIA: No. He was at war. He is the general. He only likes Spanish food. He will be here for several weeks. Maybe even a month. It depends on the situation.

SUSANNA: There is a situation?

ALICIA: Don't play the village idiot with me, Susanna. You know the situation. Do you think Juana can make Spanish food?

SUSANNA: Juana has left, Señora.

ALICIA: What do you mean she has left?

SUSANNA: She has disappeared.

ALICIA: When did she leave?

SUSANNA: A few weeks ago.

ALICIA: Well what about Han?

SUSANNA: Han was trained to cook by Juana. But she was not a good cook. She was very young when she came here, you know. She gets rose petals for your bath, she has a beautiful smile. She can't cook a whole meal, Señora. She only knows how to cook sweet things. I don't think she learned how to cook anything in China. She makes *treats*, not *food*. She helps butcher the lambs and pigs. She's not really a cook, Señora.

ALICIA: We will have to find a Spanish cook.

SUSANNA: But, Señora, it is very difficult to find a Spanish cook these days.

ALICIA: We will have to look. We cannot have an African cook.

SUSANNA: How about an Indian?

ALICIA: *(Pause.)* We will tell him that Han is the cook. He'll never know the truth. He'll never come into the kitchen.

ALICIA: *(Of the* GIRL.*)* Why is she staring at me?

SUSANNA: She thinks you are beautiful, Señora.

ALICIA: What is her name?

SUSANNA: She does not have a name, Señora.

ALICIA: Everyone has a name. What is your name?

SUSANNA: She does not know her name, Señora.

ALICIA: Carlito wants to know her name.

SUSANNA: Her mother did not tell me. And this girl cannot speak. Her mother is named Sidi. Perhaps we should call her by her mother's name. *(She faces the* GIRL.*)* Sidi!

(The GIRL *does not respond.)*

ALICIA: That is not her name. We will call her Rosa, for the lovely woman who was my nurse. You know Rosa?

SUSANNA: I remember her.

ALICIA: The saints bless her. Come with me. We will talk to the cook.

(ALICIA *exits.* SUSANNA *looks back at the child.*)

SUSANNA: Rosa!

(*The* GIRL *jumps, then moves toward* SUSANNA.)

Aha! You know your name. No! Stay. Stay. Work. Clean the floor beside the lion's feet. His claws are hurting from the dirt. This dirt will make him sick.

(*The* GIRL *goes back under the piano.*)

Scene 8

(Two months later.)

(MARTINE, EDUARDO, ALICIA, and ANTONIO are seated in the sitting area, stage right. ANTONIO is shorter and fatter than EDUARDO. He wears an 1896 (pre–Spanish-American War) Spanish general's army uniform. CARLITO enters carrying his cello and some sheet music. ALICIA, EDUARDO, and ANTONIO applaud.)

EDUARDO: I see you have come to your senses. You bring your music to the performance now! No mistakes for Uncle Antonio, eh? No mistakes for the general!

(CARLITO goes to the music stand without even the slightest flicker of response on his face.)

ALICIA: He doesn't really need it. He knows every piece in his heart. He has the spirit of your grandfather. And my great-grandfather. Susanna says he has the spirit of—

EDUARDO: Ssssh. He is about to begin.

(TEDDY sneaks in quietly just as he is beginning.)

(CARLITO plays a solo from the Brahms Cello Concerto in D Major, opus 77. SUSANNA and ROSA enter carrying trays of refreshments. SUSANNA has tall drinks on her tray. ROSA is carrying a tray of hors d'oeuvres. CHAN is carrying refreshments too. They stand behind ANTONIO and EDUARDO. As CARLITO finishes his selection, the three adults applaud. ANTONIO's applause is the loudest and longest.)

ANTONIO: Beautiful!!!! Beautiful music! (*Without looking around, he reaches for something to eat from* ROSA's *tray. He waves his hand up and down until he finds the tray, adjusting to* ROSA's *height.*) But, may I ask, who is the composer? Of this beautiful music?

(EDUARDO *absently reaches around for a drink and something to eat. First he has to raise his arms high to find* SUSANNA's *tray.* SUSANNA *signals* ROSA *to come forward. He then adjusts, reaching low for* ROSA's *tray.*)

ALICIA: The composer is Brahms.

ANTONIO: The German?

MARTINE: He was living in Vienna.

ANTONIO: What am I eating?

ALICIA: Antonio, we will try to have a Spanish cook as soon as possible. We could not find one so quickly. They are harder to find in Cuba right now. I am very, very sorry, because I know how much you like to have a Spanish kitchen wherever you are.

ANTONIO: But what is this?

EDUARDO: It is something the Negroes make, Antonio. We like it very much. It is made of good Cuban cornmeal. And, I believe, it was Alicia's grandfather, yes? Who had it made. The Negroes made it on one of his birthdays. Isn't that right?

ALICIA: It was the mistress of my grandfather. She invented it especially for him on one of his birthdays.

ANTONIO: And your grandfather had a mistress who was a Negro?

ALICIA: This is the story I have been told.

ANTONIO: And who told you this story?

ALICIA: It was Susanna.

ANTONIO: Who?

SUSANNA: It was I, Señor. Who told her the story.

ANTONIO: And now, the cooks in your house are African?

(TEDDY *glances at* SUSANNA, *who meets her gaze and comes over to her.* TEDDY *whispers something to her.* SUSANNA *tells* CHAN *something.* CHAN *leaves the room.*)

ALICIA: The cook is Chinese, but she makes Cuban food. This treat is just something special. I didn't know she would make it.

EDUARDO: He makes a mixture of food, hermano.

ANTONIO: I would like to talk to your cook. If my soldiers can cook Spanish food in the fields, this cook of yours can too. I will show her how, and then you will have some good Spanish food while Uncle Antonio is here, eh, Carlito?

EDUARDO: Susanna, go and get Han.

(SUSANNA *exits.*)

ANTONIO: But, Carlito. Play us something more. Perhaps a zarzuela or a flamenco.

CARLITO: The cello is not the same as a guitar.

EDUARDO: Carlito! Don't be so naughty when you speak to Uncle Antonio. I am surprised at you.

ANTONIO: Let him speak! I like this. Enh-henh.

(SUSANNA *reenters with* HAN. ANTONIO *rises.*)

ANTONIO: So you are the cook.

HAN: Yes, Señor.

ANTONIO: Chinese?

HAN: No, Señor. Cuban.

ANTONIO: I certainly don't want to eat *Cuban* food. True, I have eaten it when I visited you before, but you couldn't possibly expect me to eat it now. Under the circumstances. These crazy Cubans and their rebellion from Spain! I could be poisoned!

ALICIA: Really, Antonio. *I* am Cuban. Do you suggest I would poison you? (*Slight giggle.*)

ANTONIO: You say you are Cuban, but you are not a cook. We're talking about cooks. Besides, as far as I am concerned, you are Spanish. I studied your genealogy very carefully when you were courting Eduardo! You are *pure-blood* Spanish! Born in Cuba, perhaps, but *full-blood* Spanish! Do you think we would have allowed anything else to carry a Lopez y Vargas? No! It was *a pure* Spanish womb! That carried Carlito!

ALICIA: But, Antonio, I think your genealogy is ridiculous. My mother was born here, my father was born here, my grandfather was born here, my great-grand——

(EDUARDO *laughs.*)

ANTONIO: No offense, Alicia, to your kitchen, but Eduardo will tell you, African food has never agreed with me. It's too . . . strange for a man like me. I like to know what I am eating. Cuban food has that African influence.

(CHAN *reenters with a cigarette for* TEDDY. *He steps forward and lights it for her.*)

ANTONIO: And who is this lovely lady sitting here with the porcelain skin and the shiny dark hair?

ALICIA: Oh! This is Teddy, Theodora, my dear friend from college.

(SUSANNA *exits.*)

ANTONIO: This is the American college that you attended? Or the British college that you attended?

ALICIA: The American one.

ANTONIO: So you are an American?

TEDDY: I am.

ANTONIO: Unh-hunh. And is it the custom that women in America smoke cigarettes?

TEDDY: Yes, it is the custom. For a certain type of woman. Is it the custom in Spain?

ANTONIO: For a certain type of woman. Yes. And what kind of woman smokes cigarettes in America, may I ask?

TEDDY: A free woman. And what type of woman smokes cigarettes in Spain?

ANTONIO: A loose woman.

TEDDY: There is a difference between free and loose.

ANTONIO: Yes, but not enough of a difference for my satisfaction. Let me say that in Spain it is a woman for hire who smokes cigarettes.

TEDDY: There are all kinds of hire.

ANTONIO: Then let me say specifically it is the type of woman who is hired to please a man's basest desires.

MARTINE: We get your point.

(MONROE *enters.*)

MONROE: I bring good news!! Very good news!!! I managed to get a wire to come through!!! Finally I have managed to get a wire to come through, right here in your house, on the outskirts of Santiago de Cuba. It's a victory!

(*Silence.*)

ANTONIO: And may I ask who you are?

(Pause.)

ALICIA: Eduardo. Didn't you introduce Antonio to Monroe? Didn't you tell him about our guest, Monroe, when you took your long ride around the plantation and into the hills? I would have thought they would have met by now.

EDUARDO: Antonio, this is Monroe, from the States. He is traveling with Theodora.

ANTONIO: He is your servant? And he bursts into the room speaking in the midst of our conversation? Now that you finally ended slavery, you cannot control your servants in America?

TEDDY: He is not my servant.

EDUARDO: You would be interested, Antonio. He can do anything that has to do with wires. He put an electrical system in the stables. You have no idea how helpful it was when our new calf was born last week. He is the protégé of Edison.

ANTONIO: Of who?

EDUARDO: Of the man who invented electricity, Thomas Edison.

ANTONIO: That American who stole his ideas from elsewhere? He didn't invent electricity. He put a glass case around something that was natural. And produced millions of them. That's America. They make cases, packages. For everything. And then they multiply what they make. Multiply, multiply.

(HAN comes over to MONROE with something to eat.)

ANTONIO: Is he to be served here just like the rest of us?

(Pause.)

ALICIA: Eduardo, I think you could explain it better than I.

EDUARDO: My brother. Really. We of Lopez y Vargas were trained above all else, whether farmers or warriors, to be gentlemen.

ANTONIO: *(Stands.)* We were trained to be gentlemen among gentlemen.

ALICIA: Monroe appears to us to be the model of a gentleman. That is how he looks to us, through our eyes.

ANTONIO: I asked only. Is he to be served here just like the rest of us?

(Pause.)

EDUARDO: Yes, he is.

ANTONIO: I see.

ALICIA: Teddy. Monroe. I appreciate your patience while we clarified a few things for Antonio.

ANTONIO: Is it suddenly a crime, to want to clarify the habits of a culture? I am a warrior, I like to know the terrain. I only wanted to know. Is he to be *served* like us? Will he *dine* with us?

ALICIA: We are all *"us,"* Antonio.

ANTONIO: The last time I was here you still had slaves. Alicia. Your father had slaves in the field, he had them in the

house, he had them everywhere. So don't be so much like
the bishop of the church with me! I only wanted it to be
clear! I apologize. Monroe, and . . . Teddy, if I have been
insulting.

(ANTONIO *sits.* MARTINE *starts to play the Chopin waltz [Chopin,
"Grand Valse Brillante," opus 34, number 2], taking his cue from*
ALICIA, *who nods.)*

Scene 9

(CARLITO's cello is lying, out of its case, on the piano bench. ROSA is scrubbing.)

(ROSA rises and stands next to the music stand. She walks over to the bench and stands staring at CARLITO's cello.)

SUSANNA *(Entering.)* Don't touch that!!!!

(ROSA jumps.)

> Do not touch the cello! And do not touch the stick which Carlito uses to play the cello. If you touch the stick which Carlito uses to play the cello, it will jump and cut your throat like a machete!

(SUSANNA plucks a string of the cello. ROSA jumps.)

> Aha!!! I see you know one Spanish word! Machete!

(ROSA jumps.)

> Machete!

(ROSA jumps.)

> Ave Maria! You know one Spanish word! *(Pause.)* Machete! *(She laughs.)* So! I caught you. I caught you understanding Spanish! At least one word. Where did you learn *machete*? From Carlito? From Chan? Who taught you?

(ROSA *does not respond.*)

It's all right. *(Pause.)* Yes, little criolitta, little mulatta. It's all right. Come.

Scene 10

(ANTONIO *and* EDUARDO *are playing chess.* ALICIA *is at the piano playing Louis Moreau Gottschalk's "Pasquinade."* MARTINE *is with her. She plays carefully and repeats some small portion of the piece. She is dressed to go shopping. [Second movement of Mac-Dowell suite, "Andantino and Allegretto."]* ROSA *is behind her scrubbing.* CARLITO *and* SUSANNA *enter, also dressed to go shopping.* TEDDY *is reading.*)

MARTINE: No. No. No. That's not it.

CARLITO: Mami. The horses are ready.

ALICIA: Teddy, shall we? We are going to buy some lace. Come with us, Martine. I can use your opinion.

(ALICIA *takes him by the arm, locking elbows.*)

ANTONIO: If I had known you needed some lace, I would have brought you some beautiful lace from Madrid.

ALICIA: The curtains on the long windows are decaying. They need new lace.

(*She exits with* MARTINE, *elbow to elbow.* CARLITO, TEDDY, *and* SUSANNA *leave also. The sound of* ROSA's *scrubbing is heard. The chess game is at a standstill.*)

ANTONIO: She takes that music master with her wherever she goes. What is he, her lapdog? Actually that's not a bad position for a man, to be a woman's lapdog. It's not a position I would want, but for a certain type of man, it might be fun. A lapdog. Is he her lapdog, or something more? Eduardo! Doesn't it trouble you that she takes him wherever she goes?

EDUARDO: Who? What? What are you grumbling about now, Antonio?

ANTONIO: If you are not going to make your move, at least knock the ash off of your cigar, it will fall off.

EDUARDO: Thank you.

ANTONIO: Does the girl scrub the floor every day?

EDUARDO: It is very dusty here. The hills are so near us. The dust does not stay in the hills, you know. The dust loves to come down from the hills and visit us. To tell you the truth I think it is the dust that has decayed Alicia's lace. She has to buy new lace almost every year. And think of it, Antonio, in the summer house, in Málaga, we still have the same lace that we have had for many years.

ANTONIO: It is hard to keep your old things when you leave your country. And I told you that, years ago. (Pause.) But where is the mother of this child?

EDUARDO: The mother of the girl? You mean Rosa? This girl here?

ANTONIO: I would like to meet her mother. If you could arrange it. Arrange for me to meet the mother. If someone knows where she is. Pretty little girl.

EDUARDO: She is pretty because she is Spanish. Look carefully. It's the Spanish that makes her pretty! Want me to arrange for you to meet the Spanish? That's her father! If it's pretty you want, I will arrange a rendezvous with her papa.

ANTONIO: She is not Spanish.

EDUARDO: I happen to know for a fact that she is Spanish!

ANTONIO: I see, personal. Do you mean to tell me that I am looking at my niece???

EDUARDO: No, not that. Believe it or not, I am faithful.

ANTONIO: Oh, come on, my brother! We all know you are a hopeless romantic, but I hope you are not a dolt. Alicia is very beautiful, that's true. But faithful to her? You? Totally? You, a Lopez y Vargas?

EDUARDO: Not Alicia. To my mistress. I am very faithful to my mistress. I have only one. The entire time that I have been in Cuba. I love her. I am devoted. I think I am crazy.

(*The sound of* ROSA's *scrubbing is heard. She goes under the piano. Pause.*)

It is your move now.

ANTONIO: And how old is your mistress?

EDUARDO: She is young.

ANTONIO: So how old was she when you got her? You have been living in Cuba for ten years.

EDUARDO: Why all these questions?

ANTONIO: But how young? How young was she when you took her?

EDUARDO: It is good to take a mistress when she is young. If you plan to keep her it is good, because you can train her.

(CHAN *comes to the door.*)

CHAN: We have cleaned your guns now.

EDUARDO: Good!!! (*He stands.*)

ANTONIO: (*He stands, lingers over the chess table.*) Aha! (*He makes his move.*)

EDUARDO: (ANTONIO *turns to stare at* ROSA, *who is under the piano.*) Really, Antonio. She is too young. Besides, you have no intention of being around to watch her grow. And when they are this young, they do not have the flame yet. The flame of challenge. It is only a battle with their fear. Seldom their will. It isn't interesting. It's rather boring. Flat. Like wash water.

ANTONIO: Well. On second thought, why waste my seed on an African?

(*They exit,* ANTONIO *giving* EDUARDO *an almost paternal touch on the back as they go.* ROSA *continues to scrub. After a moment she goes to each window and peers out. Then she goes to the piano. She plays an exact copy of* ALICIA's *rendition of Gottschalk's "Pasquinade," cautious and careful.*)

Scene 11

(ROSA *is scrubbing the floor.* SUSANNA *is taking dying roses out of a vase and putting fresh ones in. She takes the petals off the dying roses and puts them in a bowl.*)

(CHAN *enters with a book.*)

SUSANNA: *(Exasperated.)* Where have you been?!

CHAN: I was talking to Señora Theodora.

SUSANNA: I sent for you an hour ago!

CHAN: Emiliano, who was ringing the bells, has joined the insurrectos. We can't depend on the bells anymore! Susanna, you know as well as I do!

SUSANNA: Don't talk to me that way. "Susanna, you know as well as I do!" I would suggest that you learn to tell time without the bells. Those of us who have lived here for generations know how to do that, and I would suggest that you learn how to do it!

CHAN: I got lost in the conversation with Señora Theodora!

SUSANNA: *(Barely letting him finish.)* Rosa, go!

(ROSA *leaves.*)

I am your master in this house. Not Señora Theodora. She is a guest! You answer to me, as all the servants have for years! Servants who were finer "revolutionaries than you." Do you understand?

CHAN: All right . . .

SUSANNA: What?

CHAN: Yes, Susanna.

SUSANNA: Say that again.

CHAN: Yes, Susanna.

(Pause.)

SUSANNA: There has been a killing.

CHAN: Who?

SUSANNA: One of the high priests of our religion was killed. He was one of the main servants of Chango. He was shot by a Spanish firing squad. Many saw the killing.

CHAN: (Enraged.) Bastards!

(Pause.)

SUSANNA: I think my people are ready to join yours.

CHAN: What did you say?

SUSANNA: My people are ready to join yours.

CHAN: This is wonderful news!

SUSANNA: That a priest was killed? It's not wonderful news. Not wonderful news at all!

CHAN: Good news! You're finally ready to get the Spaniards out of here!

SUSANNA: We're not "finally" ready. I don't appreciate you coming in here acting as though this is the first time we have tried to get the Spaniards out of here! We Cubans have been working very hard at this for years! And you have no appreciation. No appreciation!

CHAN: What's different this time are the ideas.

SUSANNA: I don't care so much about your ideas. The blood flows the same. Get back to work. I only wanted you to know that we are ready for a meeting. I will bring my people if you will bring yours. Just after midnight tonight. The old barn in the east hills.

(Pause.)

What is that book?

CHAN: *The Writings of José Martí.*

SUSANNA: And you say that Theodora gave it to you?

CHAN: What do you care? You can't read.

SUSANNA: What is Señora Theodora doing with a book like that? You trust these Americans?

(Pause.)

CHAN: It's Señora Theodora. I know her very well. I've known her for years.

SUSANNA: So have I. She is an American.

(HAN *enters.*)

HAN: Señora Alicia is waiting for the rose petals to put them in her bath.

(SUSANNA *gives* HAN *the rose petals.*)

Scene 12

(ROSA *is scrubbing the floor.* ALICIA *is playing the piano: the Andantino and Allegretto of MacDowell's* First Modern Suite. MARTINE *is watching.*)

(*She now plays it with great ease and authority.* ANTONIO *enters in military uniform, wearing a double holster with two pistols in it.*)

(ALICIA *rises.*)

ANTONIO: Continue. Continue.

ALICIA: How was your morning?

ANTONIO: Things are better left in the mouths of the old lady gossips. As for me, my mouth remains manly and shut!

ALICIA: Does Eduardo know that you are back?

ANTONIO: Yes. Yes. Play. Play.

(*She sits and continues to play.* ANTONIO *lights a cigar.* EDUARDO *enters.* ALICIA *stops abruptly and rises.*)

But why do you stand?

ALICIA: I can tell that the two of you would like to talk.

ANTONIO: (*Reaches for a sweet from a dish on one of the tables.*) We can go someplace else. You know I am going to get fat here. Everywhere you go there is a sugared treat.

ALICIA: Excuse me.

ANTONIO: But tell me, Alicia. Who was the composer?

ALICIA: It was MacDowell.

ANTONIO: A Scots? I never heard of a Scots composer.

ALICIA: He is American.

ANTONIO: But why don't you play some Spanish music in this house?

(*Without turning around,* ALICIA *picks up the music from the piano, holds it high above her head, and lets it fall all over the floor.*)

(ROSA *is scrubbing the floor.*)

ALICIA: Martine, I suppose you should find me some Spanish music. If the General is planning to stay much longer. The problem Antonio, is that very little Spanish music of this time is composed for the piano. You Spaniards prefer the guitar.

(*She exits.*)

ANTONIO: Why is your wife playing American music?

MARTINE: It is I who am responsible for what she plays.

EDUARDO: Really, Martine, don't take the blame. My wife is very willful.

ANTONIO: First this Viennese, this German, and that Frenchman. I can understand that. Everyone plays those. Even in Spain. But this American with a Scottish name?

MARTINE: It's easy enough to play Spanish music. We will try Albéniz.

ANTONIO: *(Cutting him off.)* And her clothing! It's getting cheaper and gaudier by the day.

EDUARDO: Teddy has brought her many new things from New York.

ANTONIO: Who?

EDUARDO: Teddy? Her American friend?

ANTONIO: You mean Desdemona? With her titties like ripe peaches? I would squeeze her peaches in my hands but I lost interest in her the minute her Moor appeared. What a carnival your house has become, my brother.

ANTONIO: *(To* MARTINE.*)* Do you mind leaving me alone with my brother, so that I can speak with him man to man?

(MARTINE *begins to pick up the music that* ALICIA *has left.*)

(ANTONIO *walks over and takes it from him, dropping it back onto the floor.*)

Leave the music! And leave us alone!

(MARTINE *leaves.*)

(Calling after him.) And grow some balls while you're gone!

(To EDUARDO.) He's like one of those eunuchs in the ancient temples! I can't stand simpering people. "It is I who am responsible for what she plays." I'm sick of talking about music when there's a war coming!

EDUARDO: I can tell that the news is not good.

ANTONIO: Very bad news. These bloodthirsty thieves, your "insurrectos," your "revolutionaries," and now their new friends, the Americans, think they are going to win this war! My spies tell me that Roosevelt had the nerve to say that he was going to shove Spain out of the Americas! Oh really! Oh *really?*

(ANTONIO *throws a couple of sugared treats from a dish nearby into his mouth.)*

And look at me! I can't even stop eating these sugared treats! I'm losing my own manhood in this house! *(He spits the treats at the floor and then sits. Pause.)* I need you to continue your hospitality. This house has the best position from which to work, if it is possible, my brother.

EDUARDO: You are my brother, and I care as much about Spain as you do.

ANTONIO: I am glad to hear it, because sometimes I wonder about your loyalty.

EDUARDO: Don't be loco.

ANTONIO: But can you imagine! To shove Spain out of the Americas? We got here first. *(Rising.)*

EDUARDO: But those kinds of statements, my brother, how can

you take them seriously? They only make the newspapermen richer.

ANTONIO: You wouldn't know because you have never fought.
And, my brother, perhaps you should consider fighting in
this war! *(Pause. He laughs loudly.)*

I am only joking!

EDUARDO: What, you don't think I have the stomach?

ANTONIO: I am the warrior, you are the farmer. *(He grabs
EDUARDO roughly by the head and neck and then kisses him
on the lips.)*

(Pause.)

(CARLITO enters with his cello, and with SUSANNA.)

ANTONIO: Oh! Our little Mozart!

CARLITO: Where is my mother?

ANTONIO: She and her music master are trying on dresses in the
garden.

EDUARDO: Come, Carlito, Uncle Antonio is only joking.

ANTONIO: I want to show you something special, Carlosito.

SUSANNA: Carlito! Go to your uncle. He wants to show you something.

ANTONIO: Susanna. Don't you have some washing to do?

SUSANNA: No, Señor, I train others to do the washing.

ANTONIO: Well take a rest then, and leave Carlito to us.

EDUARDO: It's all right, Susanna.

(SUSANNA *leaves.*)

ANTONIO: What do you think of my guns?

(Pause.)

I bet you and your father don't have these types of guns here in Cuba. Here, you can hold it. Go ahead.

Don't be shy. It's not so hard to use this kind of gun.

EDUARDO: But this is not the place to shoot a gun, Antonio.

ANTONIO: Here, Carlosito.

(He puts the gun into CARLITO's *hand.)*

Give your arm some strength! Come on! Give it some force! Here! Try again!

(ROSA *enters carrying the bucket.)*

What kinds of guns are you used to?

EDUARDO: He has never held a gun.

ANTONIO: Never held a gun! Well it's a good thing that Uncle Antonio has come, so that you can learn from the master!

Never held a gun! But give it back, because you can't hold it like that. Now try holding it like this.

EDUARDO: It's all right to try, Carlito.

ANTONIO: That's no way to talk about guns, Eduardo! "It's all right to try!" There are too many women around this boy. Talk to him like a man! Carlito! Take the gun!

(CARLITO *does not move.*)

If you can hold your cello, which is as full and round as a woman, you can hold this gun! Here, hold this. Hold it! It's only a pistol. Small enough for a woman. I know your balls are not very big. But these are the things that will make them grow. To have big balls in this day and age is even more important than to have a mother and a father. I loved my mother, your grandmam, and I loved my father, but I love my balls more than anything, because without them, I cannot think for myself what I want to do with my own life.

(CARLITO *takes the gun.*)

Thank God for Uncle Antonio, eh? How disgusting that a boy your age hasn't been taken out to hunt. What on earth will they do when it's time to show you the ladies?

(CARLITO *takes the gun.*)

Eduardo! I am amazed that he has never held a gun! Not even to shoot a rabbit?

(CARLITO *drops the gun and starts to run out of the room.*)

Where do you think you are going? That's a stupid thing to do, to drop a gun! You could have killed us all! Dropping a gun!

EDUARDO: Antonio, let him go, he's only a boy.

ANTONIO: Let me take care of this! I have broken horses and I can break this boy!

(ANTONIO *goes after* CARLITO.)

EDUARDO: Really, my brother, I have broken more horses than you have!

(ANTONIO *gets* CARLITO *and brings him, by force, back into the room.*)

ANTONIO: Never drop a gun! Never! Now you have a choice! You can play the cello and the piano, and you can end up like your mother and her music teacher, wearing dresses, or you can hold this gun and be like the rest of us.

EDUARDO: Really, Antonio, his music teacher does not wear a dress.

ANTONIO: Are you listening to me, Carlito? Nobody likes a man who does not act like a man.

CARLITO: Susanna says I act like a man.

ANTONIO: But Susanna is an animal. She is not a full person. She is not a full person.

CARLITO: Yes she is.

ANTONIO: Trust me. She is from Africa, like the apes, she is not a full person. If she lifted her dress you would see that she does not have what women have, she has what apes have. Now what's the matter with you? Why can't you hold this gun? Oh, now are you crying? You aren't crying, are you? Why can't you hold this gun!!!!! I never met a boy who couldn't hold a gun!!! Your papi and I were holding guns when we were six years old!

(CHAN *enters.*)

EDUARDO: My brother, that's enough!

ANTONIO: No, I'm not finished. He's crying!!!!! He plays the cello, he plays the piano, and now he's playing with tears. It won't work!

EDUARDO: (*Sharply.*) What is it, Chan?

CHAN: The men in the stable came to say that mare is having trouble. She is giving birth—

EDUARDO: My brother, we will have to finish this later. One of my horses is giving birth!

ANTONIO: (*Looking at* ROSA.) What is the girl staring at?

EDUARDO: Perhaps she has never seen a gun!

ANTONIO: Highly unlikely. Look at how she watches the gun! Too bad. Our only Lopez y Vargas is afraid to hold a gun, and this girl is fascinated. But why don't you teach the girl not to stare? It's not right.

EDUARDO: I have to go, my brother! Come with me! Chan! Where is Susanna? Isn't it time for Carlito to have lunch?

CHAN: Emiliano who rings the bells has disappeared.

EDUARDO: I don't care about the bells! It is time for Carlito to have his lunch! Antonio come!

ANTONIO: You can't escape this, Carlito. One day you will have to hold this gun! It won't go away.

(ANTONIO *leaves.* ROSA *and* CHAN *are staring at* CARLITO.)

CARLITO: I hate my uncle.

CHAN: That may be true. But what are you going to do about it? Tell your mother?

CARLITO: She won't do anything.

CHAN: That's right. Then perhaps you could tell Susanna.

CARLITO: She won't do anything.

CHAN: I can see you understand the situation. And your father?

CARLITO: He didn't do anything.

CHAN: Your uncle says you will never be a man. I think there's only one thing a man has to do to be a man. Know what that is? All you have to do to be a man is keep your mouth shut. All you have to do is show that you can keep stories, if you are told to keep them quiet. I can tell you some stories about your uncle if you show me what a man you are.

CARLITO: How do I do that?

CHAN: I am going to tell you one thing about your uncle. Something that will explain to you what he is. And if you can keep it quiet, I will tell you more.

CARLITO: I can be quiet.

CHAN: All right. Your uncle is a coward. I saw him shoot a man in the head, with his gun just like this pointed just right here at the side of his temple, because the man would not say what Antonio wanted him to say. He did this while the children of the man watched. And then he shot their mother. *(Pause.)* And then he shot the baby child because the baby was crying. *(Pause.)* He wants to control the people, just like he was trying to control you. But he will never control you because you are strong. Now. That's all for today.

CARLITO: Tell me more.

CHAN: I won't tell you any more until you show me you can keep that a secret.

*(*MARTINE *enters.)*

*(*MARTINE *picks up the music.)*

CHAN: General Antonio has departed to the stables.

MARTINE: It seems as if he decided to forgo the stables. Now he is in the kitchen. Making Han serve him as if he were a king.

(CHAN *rushes off.*)

MARTINE: Let's do your lesson.

CARLITO: I don't feel like it.

MARTINE: Don't worry about your uncle. You can shoot a gun.
Anyone can shoot a gun. I'll take you to the hills tomorrow
and we will shoot guns, but now, let's play the piano. This is
the best time to play the piano, when our hearts are open.
Sometimes, when your heart is wounded it is free. I love to
sing when my heart is hurting. That is the most beautiful
music in the world. The music of the wound, the music of
the open heart. The pig is in the kitchen eating. Oh yes,
Carlito, I understand. He's a pig. Besides, Rosa loves it when
we play the piano. Right, Rosa?

(*A different section of the Chopin waltz, opus 34, number 2, is
played, starting at measure 16.*)

Scene 13

(SUSANNA *enters carrying a very large ladder. She is followed by* ROSA, *who is weighed down with lace. There is a huge crate in the middle of the floor.*)

SUSANNA: Put the lace down on the couch.

(ROSA *suddenly jumps.* CHAN *is coming in through the French windows.*)

You are too high-strung.

CHAN: I have to talk to you.

SUSANNA: What do you mean coming in here like a bandit? Use the door.

Rosa! Go!

(ROSA *exits.*)

CHAN: I have someone who is here to see you.

SUSANNA: Don't take all day. I have work to do.

(CHAN *leaves and reenters with* OCHO, *an African man.*)

OCHO: Hello, Mami.

SUSANNA: What are you doing here?

OCHO: I am your eighth son. You are my mother. Don't you like a visit?

CHAN: I've tried to tell you that Ocho is a hero in the revolution and you won't believe me. Seeing is believing.

SUSANNA: Heroes in the revolution end up shot full of bullets!

OCHO: You were a revolutionary when you were young.

SUSANNA: But the guns are different now!

OCHO: Mami, do you know that the general is rounding up people around here and putting them into reconcentrados?

SUSANNA: Reconcentrados?

CHAN: Concentration camps. This General Antonio, this "Lopez y Vargas." He is here only a few weeks and already the insurrectos have cause to spit at the sound of his name.

OCHO: Now that they have put reconcentrados, here, near Santiago, they will move all the way up the inside lands.

SUSANNA: Reconcentrados?

CHAN: Pens, full of people. Cages. That's right. And he is taking thousands. Cattle too.

OCHO: Do Eduardo and Alicia know about this?

SUSANNA: They are in another world. They live in a fantasy.

OCHO: Mami, I would suggest you pack your things and come with me. I can keep you safe in the hills.

SUSANNA: I have kept myself safe all these years, why would I need to do that?

OCHO: We are going to burn the house tomorrow.

SUSANNA: You cannot burn this house!!!!!! We cannot burn this house without permission from Chango.

OCHO: Before you know it, he will put you in the reconcentrado.

SUSANNA: Listen to me. I can practically read his mind. Just give me a few more full moons, and I will know his every plan, and so will you. Now is not the time.

(CHAN *and* OCHO *run out of the garden doors as* ANTONIO *enters.*)

ANTONIO: Ah! The crate has arrived for me. (SUSANNA *proceeds to hang the lace curtains.*) I need something to open it. Where is your machete?

SUSANNA: I don't have a machete, Señor.

ANTONIO: Where is Chan?

SUSANNA: I have not seen him today, Señor.

ANTONIO: Go and get me a machete.

(SUSANNA *exits.* ANTONIO *lights a cigar.* CARLITO *enters carrying his cello.* TEDDY *follows. She sits with a book and a cigarette. Smoking and reading.*)

Our little Mozart!

(CARLITO *sets up his music. He plucks out a gypsy tune on the cello.*)

Well, well, well. I feel so much hospitality. Just as requested! You are learning some gypsy tunes.

(SUSANNA *reenters carrying a machete.* ROSA *is at her heels with the bucket. She begins to scrub the floor.* ANTONIO *takes the machete from* SUSANNA.)

"Providence, Rhode Island!!!" Can you read, Susanna?! This machete says, "Providence, Rhode Island." These Americans. They have no class. They send you machetes and they write on them "Providence, Rhode Island"? Don't they know a person like me can read English?

(*He blasts the crate open with the machete. There are guns in the crate.* CARLITO *runs out.* SUSANNA *is taking the old curtains down.*)

(ANTONIO *turns to* ROSA, *his gun hanging at the side of his thigh in one hand and his other arm held straight out with a finger pointed very directly at her. She jumps.*)

Don't stare! (*Pause.*) Enh-henh! Don't stare. It's wrong.

(*He laughs as she jumps again.* ROSA *and* SUSANNA *leave.*)

(ANTONIO *goes over to* TEDDY *and takes her cigarette out of her hand. He takes a drag.*)

So. How would you like to make history with me?

(*Pause.*)

Let's make history. There are not very many instances where
a woman like you would make love to a man like me.

(Pause.)

So let's make history.

(Pause.)

I thought you might be crazy enough to like a guy like
Antonio.

TEDDY: I'm not crazy at all actually.

ANTONIO: Are you a spy?

TEDDY: Would I tell you if I were?

ANTONIO: Women. You're talking too much these days. I liked it
better when you didn't have so much to say. Anyway— You
don't know what you're missing. With a man like me. I may
not be to your liking, but that's where you women make
your mistake, being so attracted to dandies, rather than warriors. You'll never know what you're missing.

(He leaves.)

Scene 14

(MARTINE *is playing the piano. He is practicing something rather difficult.* [*Granados, Spanish Dances Number 2, "Oriental."*] *There is a lot of repetition.* HAN *is hanging lace. She climbs a ladder and hangs pieces of lace from the window frames.* MARTINE *finds his stride, and the two of them seem almost to be in a ballet together, her movements and his music.* ANTONIO *enters with a large map and spreads it out on the table. He looks at the map and looks up at* HAN. *He watches her every move. It is aesthetically very pleasing against the music.*)

ANTONIO: Who is the composer?

(MARTINE *rises and leaves.* ANTONIO *attends to his map and then he goes to* HAN. *Helps her down from the ladder.*)

ANTONIO: And now for my basest desires. You! Such a lovely lady to receive my basest desires.

(*With each "my basest desires," he attempts to kiss her.*)

My basest desires. My basest desires. My basest desires.

(*He rapes her.*)

Scene 15

*(*SUSANNA, CHAN, HAN, OCHO, *and* MARTINE *are alone.)*

*(*SUSANNA *and* CHAN *are seated in chairs, facing the piano, as others have sat previously to watch* ALICIA, CARLITO, *and* MARTINE *perform.* HAN *is sitting on the piano bench.)*

CHAN: I will kill him. I will kill him!

SUSANNA: You can't kill him. We need him alive.

CHAN: I will kill him, and I will burn the house.

SUSANNA: You can't burn the house.

CHAN: Let's blow the roof off the house!

SUSANNA: Something will blow up, but not the house.

CHAN: Spare me your riddles.

*(*HAN *is seated for the first part of the speech on the piano bench.)*

(This entire speech is spoken very rapidly, but with variety. It is joyful, sad, angry. It is a tirade of the full spectrum of emotions, done with great speed, bursting out.)

HAN: I was so young when I came here.

*(*HAN *stands now, beside the piano as though she were a singer at a recital.)*

I spent my most tender years in this house. Cooking in the kitchen. Shining the copper pots. Washing the porcelain bowls. Pouring milk for Carlito, for his mama, and for Eduardo. My master. Pouring milk and adding sugar. Making special treats. With sugar. This treat, that treat, every treat. With sugar. Smell my hands.

(She rises and orders SUSANNA.*)*

Smell them! They smell forever sweet, forever of sugar, deep in my pores the sugar lives. And even if I go into the hills, my hands will always smell of sugar. Even after I touched the beast, my hands still smell of sugar. See?

(She thrusts her hands at CHAN.*)*

CHAN: Han, I'm so sorry I couldn't do anything to stop this from happening.

HAN: Why? My great-grandmother was raped by a man, and what did my great-grandfather do? Nothing.

(She returns to her place standing in front of the piano.)

MARTINE: I wish I. . . .

HAN: I love to welcome the guests! Don't I, Susanna?

SUSANNA: Yes, you do.

HAN: I love to welcome them. To stand outside the house on the beautiful stones, the stones that Chan shines. . . . I love to stand there in my white uniform, so fresh, so perfect, worn only for the arrivals, my "arrivals" dress. Greeting the guests.

Saying only, "Welcome to this house." And Susanna says . . .
Say what you say, Susanna!

SUSANNA: "And this is Han, let her know if there is anything you
need."

HAN: And they say to me sometimes, "What a beautiful smile
you have!" And I say nothing, I just smile.

(Pause.)

I am the only one among you who smiles!!!!!! When I serve!
I am the only one who smiles!!!!!!! Don't I get some credit
for that?????? The rest of you have no expression, standing
there holding your trays, staring ahead as if you could just as
well cut their throats as serve them. But not I. I smile. Pouring rum, pouring wine, pouring special treats, full of mint
and lemon and "special" Cuban ingredients. "Special"
Cuban ingredients!

CHAN: *(Yelling.)* Please!

HAN: And then the pigs. And the lambs. Watching the pigs
bleed, hearing them squeal when the machete hits their
heads, and taking out their stomachs, cleaning off their hair,
the hair of the pig, picking out the thick hairs of the boar.
One by one. And taking the pig, the lamb, the chicken, the
rooster, the calf, the cow . . .

OCHO: I would like to . . .

HAN: Making the garden, remaking the garden. Growing roses,
digging in the dirt so that the poppies could grow. Going

deep in the dirt and putting in the seeds for every kind of flower, helping it grow. Cutting the flowers, the purple ones, the yellow ones, the red ones, the white ones, the pink ones, the ones with a little yellow here, and a red rim around the top, the Dutch seeds, the Spanish seeds . . .

(Pause.)

Putting the fresh flowers, every day fresh, in the east hallway, the west hallway, the Señora Alicia's room, dropping rose petals in Señora Alicia's bath.

(Suddenly yelling.)

Why does she have to have rose petals in her bath!!!!!! Every—single—day?

(Pause.)

And then the slim vase for Señor Eduardo. Putting the vase of flowers beside Señor Eduardo's bath!!!! One day I forgot to put the vase beside his bath. He came into the kitchen with only a towel around his bottom, and nothing on his chest, and he screamed at me— "Where are the flowers beside my bath?"

(She laughs uncontrollably.)

"Where are the flowers beside my bath!" Putting the flowers in the slim vase, such a slim vase he likes, putting that vase with the flowers beside Señor Eduardo's bath!!!!!!

CHAN: *(Losing it.)* Stop talking about Señor Eduardo's bath!

(Lengthy pause.)

SUSANNA: This house that we have made so beautiful! Someone drew the plan many years ago, but we have kept it alive, every day, every day, every day, fixing, fixing, fixing.

We make it real. This house.

(Quietly.) What would it be without us?

(Pause.)

HAN: And this room. In this room, this very room, the animal stalks. The animal who should be kept in the stable. I say bring the horses to this room, and put that man in the stable! And we must smell his farts in the morning, no flower for him in his bath, just his cigar!

CHAN: *(Pleading.)* I would have stopped him if I could have.

(HAN sits on the bench of the piano facing them. She is perfectly erect and still. She takes the red cloth off the keys and holds it across her.)

HAN: *(Not so enraged now, more in the spirit of getting the details exactly correct.)* . . . to be on my knees while he thrust himself into me. To be on my back while he thrust himself into me. To be on my stomach while he thrust himself into me. His balls so big. These balls that he talks about all the time. And yes they are big balls. I saw them. He put them in my hand. This Lopez y Vargas forced my body to be the house of his basest desires. His basest desires. His basest desires. In the most beautiful room in the house. Rosa cannot touch the piano. But the beast touched me!

(She stops abruptly, puts the red cloth back on the keys, and moves away from the piano. We hear for ten seconds only the sound of CHAN *sobbing.)*

HAN: Why are you crying? I'm not crying. It's me who was raped, not you.

*(*CHAN *sobs.)*

*(*OCHO *suddenly flees. Beat.* TEDDY *enters. Beat.* HAN *leaves. Pause as* CHAN *continues to sob.* TEDDY *watches.)*

SUSANNA: It seems that Señor Antonio Lopez y Vargas had his way with Han.

TEDDY: His what?

SUSANNA: His way.

(Lights out.)

Scene 16

(TEDDY, ALICIA, EDUARDO, SUSANNA.)

EDUARDO: I don't believe you.

TEDDY: Why would she lie?

ALICIA: She has been working here since she was fourteen years old. I've never known her to lie. Even about the smallest detail.

EDUARDO: You're insulting my brother.

ALICIA: We're not insulting your brother.

TEDDY : Your brother is an insult to us.

EDUARDO: *(Furious.)* Get in your place Susanna, and stay there!

SUSANNA: *(Low, monotone, controlled, without emotion.)* But señor I did not speak. I did not move.

(Beat. He slaps ALICIA. *He leaves.)*

Scene 17

(EDUARDO *has his head down.* HAN *is in front of him. He does not look at her for the entire scene.*)

EDUARDO: What's your proof?

(HAN *lifts her skirt and shows her thigh.*)

HAN: I have bruises.

EDUARDO: Maybe they came from Chan.

HAN: I'm his wife. He doesn't have to rape me.

EDUARDO: Chan is very emotional.

HAN: He doesn't beat me.

EDUARDO: I can't go to my brother with this accusation.

HAN: He has a very hairy back.

EDUARDO: You could have seen him in his bath.

HAN: He has a cut on his stomach right here.

EDUARDO: In the mornings he walks in the garden with no shirt and only his suspenders, you could have seen it there. *(He grabs her arm.)*

HAN: You're hurting me.

EDUARDO: It hurts when the truth comes out. If it's true it will hurt. It's important to have the truth in matters like this. So. If it hurts, so be it. I need the truth.

(*He throws her across the room.*)

HAN: He has a mole on the inside of his thigh, very high up, near his—

EDUARDO: How do you know that?

HAN: Because he raped me!

EDUARDO: (*Losing control.*) But how do you know that! Specifically that!

HAN: Because he raped me!

(*He slaps her in the face.*)

EDUARDO: Maybe you are working with these revolutionaries, maybe you are! Tell me! How do you know that!!!!!

HAN: Because he pushed himself into my mouth, and I saw it, there, his big mole, about this big, and I will never forget it, and I will never forget how he smells! He does not smell like you. Even though you are brothers. You smell like sugar. He smells like his chamber pot.

(EDUARDO *abruptly breaks away and walks briskly out of the room.*)

(HAN *sits alone. After a beat,* HENRY *enters from the side opposite where* EDUARDO *left.*)

HENRY: Is anybody around? Hi!

(HAN *stands.*)

You're trembling. Do you have a fever?

Scene 18

(Night.)

(ANTONIO is drinking rum from a bottle and looking at sheet music. MARTINE, who has clearly been taken out of bed, enters with CHAN, who delivers him to ANTONIO. CHAN leaves.)

ANTONIO: Ah! Martine! Sorry to wake you from your sleep! Were you asleep or awake?

MARTINE: I was asleep.

ANTONIO: Ah! Well one thing warriors understand, is—there is no night and day. A real warrior is alive in the day and in the night. You look to me more like a warrior every day. Or am I imagining things?

MARTINE: You are imagining things.

ANTONIO: Enh-henh. Finally, Martine, we have something in common, you and I. You're not the only one who takes an interest in American music! I have some too! Right here! You see I have taken another tactic. I believe this music may have some useful information for me. I don't understand these lyrics. I would like you to play them and sing them for me. Let's get you some coffee! Chan!!!!!! Bring Martine some coffee!!!!!! Listen to my lungs! How loud I can be! Think I can have a place in the opera? Chan! Now!!!!!

(MARTINE takes the music and starts carefully to play out "There's A Hot Time in the Old Town Tonight" on the piano.)

ANTONIO: But sing it. I hear in the American cities they were singing this in the streets, sing it for me.

MARTINE: I'm not a singer.

ANTONIO: Well, Alicia is a singer.

MARTINE: Alicia is asleep. It's very late.

ANTONIO: *(Slamming his rum bottle.)* Then do me the honors. Sing it.

(MARTINE *cautiously begins to sing it.*)

ANTONIO: But what does this mean? "There'll be a hot time in the old town tonight."

MARTINE: I really don't know.

(ANTONIO *begins singing.*)

ANTONIO: Don't stop singing, just because I am singing. Sing with me! I want to understand this song!

(EDUARDO *comes in.*)

EDUARDO: Excuse me Martine, but I need to be alone with my brother.

(MARTINE *rises.*)

ANTONIO: But we are singing!

EDUARDO: I need to talk to you.

ANTONIO: There'll be a hot time in the old town toniiiggghttt!

(MARTINE *leaves.*)

EDUARDO: You are a Lopez y Vargas and you are a disgrace. I see you have had some ample amounts of my good Cuban rum. You smell like a distillery!

(CHAN *enters.*)

What is it, Chan?

CHAN: Señor Antonio called for coffee.

EDUARDO: He doesn't need it anymore.

(CHAN *exits.*)

ANTONIO: I might like some coffee.

EDUARDO: Shut up!

(*Pause.*)

You raped Han.

ANTONIO: Who?

EDUARDO: The beautiful woman who serves you your food, and sometimes pulls your bath for you? You raped her.

ANTONIO: Rape? What is this word *rape*? When did it start? This word *rape*. I hear those troubadours, those silly love poets in

the Middle Ages, have something to do with that word being
in our vocabulary. *Rape.* I didn't rape anyone. I only satis-
fied my basest desires. Susanna said, when I arrived: "Let
Han know if there is anything you want." I let her know. It's
that simple.

EDUARDO: *(Screaming.)* Need! Need! Susanna says "Let Han
know if there is anything you *need*!" *(Pause.)* Why does she
have bruises?

ANTONIO: It was tempestuous.

(EDUARDO stands. Goes to ANTONIO and hits him in the face.)

EDUARDO: We brothers don't steal each other's women.

ANTONIO: Just one moment, Eduardo.

(EDUARDO hits him again.)

EDUARDO: She is my mistress. The only mistress I ever had! I love
her, you understand! I love her! No! You don't understand.
You have never understood. You cannot understand about
love!

ANTONIO: Well. Now. My brother. That's not true. I love Spain.

EDUARDO: I love her as much as I love my horses! I love her as
much as I love Carlito! She is precious to me! You understand? Do—you—understand? Love! I love her! And you
ruined her!

ANTONIO: If I had known . . .

EDUARDO: You have ruined her! She will never trust me again. You have no idea how much she trusted me. You will never understand. She trusted me more than my own wife. And now there is nothing but suspicion and fear in her eyes.

ANTONIO: Women. You can never tell a woman by her eyes.

EDUARDO: How would you know? You seldom look a woman in the eyes with anything but disrespect. And if a woman looks you in the eye, you don't like it.

ANTONIO: I can look anyone in the eye. I have no problem looking anyone or anything in the eye. I have looked a lion in the eye!

EDUARDO: *(Screaming.)* We—were—not—raised—to—rape—women! Grandmama and Mama would be ashamed of you! Ashamed!

ANTONIO: Really, my brother, get your story straight. I am Antonio Lopez y Vargas, I have no problem with women, I don't need to rape a woman. I can get all the women I want!

(EDUARDO hits him again and leaves, as CARLITO enters in his nightclothes.)

CARLITO: Papi, you were yelling.

(ANTONIO sits at the piano, plays it for a few notes, and sings through the transition. Over and over.)

ANTONIO: There'll be a hot time in the old town tonight. There'll be a hot time in the old town tonight!

Scene 19

*(*ALICIA *and* TEDDY *are playing chess.)*

ALICIA: It's your move.

TEDDY: You are not going to be able to hold on to this plantation.

ALICIA: But this happened before, twenty years ago, and this
house survived all that. I have faith.

TEDDY: What are the taxes that you pay the Spanish?

ALICIA: I don't know about that. It's your move.

TEDDY: Alicia. You studied mathematics!

(Pause.)

I think you should let me buy the plantation.

ALICIA: It's your move.

TEDDY: My father has instructed me to buy as many as I can. I'm
going to buy at least ten small plantations in this area. We'll
buy yours for a generous price. *(Pause.)* I've been talking to
Eduardo about it.

ALICIA: You are like my sister, and you would talk to him about
this, knowing how much this house means to me, knowing

how I love it more than anything? You would talk to *Eduardo*? You would talk to him before talking to me?

TEDDY: It just came up in conversation. By accident. Suddenly it was so clear, so obvious.

ALICIA: *(Suddenly.)* This house is not for sale!

TEDDY: I'm trying to protect you. . . .

ALICIA: *(Standing, suddenly emotional.)* I don't need your protection! I have the protection of Chango!

TEDDY: Look, Monroe is in contact with New York every day. We know what's happening there. We know how the prices are going! And we know the future of Cuba.

ALICIA: You don't know the future of Cuba! How could you know? You are not from here!

(EDUARDO enters. ALICIA leaves.)

EDUARDO: Alicia!

(Pause.)

TEDDY: I've known her since she was four years old. I can't imagine her selling this house.

EDUARDO: And what's your offer today?

TEDDY: Let me think about it. My father can buy ten other plantations, he doesn't need to buy this one.

EDUARDO: But what would you offer today?

TEDDY: This place isn't really yours to sell.

EDUARDO: But I have influence. I can make it undesirable for her to keep it.

TEDDY: I'm not in the market anymore. Find another buyer.

EDUARDO: This is the largest in the area, and right up to the beach! I'll include my rare horses!

(She starts to leave.)

EDUARDO: Teddy! You listen to me! I don't like to be teased! You know that! This was your idea in the first place! I'll lower the price.

(TEDDY turns back to him.)

Scene 20

(MARTINE *is playing an American song,* "Take Me Out to the Ball Game." CHAN *is working.* CARLITO *is seated with* MARTINE *at the piano.*)

MARTINE: Let me go see if I can find your mother. She's late for her lesson again.

(MARTINE *leaves.*)

CARLITO: Chan. I kept my secret.

CHAN: Yes, that's right, you did.

CARLITO: So I would like another one.

CHAN: I don't have any today.

CARLITO: But how will I grow up to be a man without my secrets?

CHAN: I was thinking of taking you to the hills tomorrow to meet a famous revolutionary and to learn how to shoot, but you're not ready yet.

CARLITO: Yes I am.

CHAN: This is not a situation where you can tell your mother.

CARLITO: I know that.

CHAN: Or take your cello.

CARLITO: I've made the decision. I'm ready to leave and come with you.

CHAN: You can't even tell time. You need the bell, to tell time. And we have no bell.

CARLITO: No I don't.

CHAN: Meet me here tomorrow at three o'clock in the morning, and be ready to go with me to the hills.

CARLITO: I'll be here.

CHAN: We'll see.

Scene 21

(3:00 A.M. *the next morning. Moonlight.*)

(CARLITO *comes into the room with a small suitcase.*)

(*He sits on the piano bench.*)

(OCHO *comes in.*)

CARLITO: I am waiting for Chan.

OCHO: Come with me.

CARLITO: Am I going to the hills to meet a famous revolutionary?

OCHO: Your mother is coming into the house this very moment!
She's been out at a meeting. Let's go.

CARLITO: But I'm waiting for Chan!

OCHO: Chan will meet us! Let's go.

(*As they leave,* ROSA *runs into the room, dressed in white. She sees* CARLITO *go with* OCHO. *In a few beats,* SUSANNA *and* ALICIA *follow, dressed in white with scarves on their heads as from a Santeria ceremony.*)

Scene 22

(SUSANNA, EDUARDO, TEDDY, MONROE, ALICIA *are standing with* ROSA. EDUARDO *is holding a letter.*)

ALICIA: But what are these "reconcentrados"? What do they mean, Let the people out of the reconcentrados?

EDUARDO: Sssh. Alicia. Please. Don't speak so loudly.

ALICIA: You mean Antonio has been rounding up people like cattle and putting them in these concentration camps?

(ANTONIO *appears at the hallway doors with* CHAN *at his heels.* CHAN *does not enter the room but continues through the offstage hallway.*)

ANTONIO: Let me see the letter. *(He snatches it.)* No. You! *(To* CHAN.*)* You stay here! *(He continues reading.)* The vile bastards have kidnapped Carlosito.

(Pause.)

I will cut their balls and make their daughters lick the blood that drips into their mouths as they lie underneath the chopping block.

EDUARDO: I think the only way is to give them what they want.

ANTONIO: But what do they want? They don't even know.

ALICIA: They are asking you to release innocent people from the reconcentrados.

ANTONIO: Susanna! What can you tell me about this?

SUSANNA: Nothing, Señor.

ANTONIO: Well someone in this house knows.

(ROSA *is bolting away.* ANTONIO *grabs her roughly, and has her in his grip, as* HENRY *enters.*)

HENRY: Oh. Sorry.

ANTONIO: What do you want here?

HENRY: I just wanted everyone to know that an American battle-ship has now appeared in the harbor of Havana.

ANTONIO: For what?

HENRY: Uh. I suppose. To watch.

ANTONIO: Watch what?

(*Pause.*)

HENRY: I suppose.

ANTONIO: (*Still clutching* ROSA *in his grip.*) Watch what? (*Beat.*) We have nothing for you here. Go home. And tell your Teddy Roosevelt that he will *never* kick Spain out of the Americas. *Never!*

(ANTONIO *starts kicking at* HENRY, *still holding* ROSA *and stomping and kicking as* HENRY *backs out of the room.* HENRY *takes his pad and pen and starts jotting notes, even as he hops backward in response to* ANTONIO's *explosive stomps. Finally, with his spare hand* ANTONIO *shoots his gun at* HENRY, *just missing, and* HENRY *flees.)*

Scene 23

ALICIA: Antonio is turning my house into a military headquarters?

EDUARDO: Alicia, really.

ALICIA: This house which has been the host since 1721 of every fine person who has come to Santiago, this house who slept and fed the finest in government, the finest in art, the finest . . . This house, a military headquarters?

EDUARDO: Alicia. Don't raise your voice. Please.

ALICIA: When the Spanish flag flies here, this place becomes a walking sacrifice. Every piece of artwork, every piece of furniture, every single nook and cranny is as good as gone. It's a suicide. If the rebels don't burn this, Americans will. My son is taken because he is putting people into concentration camps? And now my house is his military *headquarters*??

EDUARDO: Please, not so loud.

ALICIA: *(Whispering.)* I say something. I say "Cuba Libre."

EDUARDO: Stop that!

ALICIA: CUBA LIBREEEEEEEE! And why aren't you doing anything about this?

EDUARDO: Susanna is waiting for you in your room. You must go to her now and pack your things.

ALICIA: Pack my things?

EDUARDO: Since the house is going to be the headquarters, it is
  better that we go to Spain.

ALICIA: You don't know anything, Eduardo.

EDUARDO: Alicia. Don't make me show Antonio that I cannot
  control my wife.

(ALICIA *laughs.*)

ALICIA: You are a dolt. A hopeless dolt! Oh, Eduardo, you are a
  cuckold to your brother's bloodthirsty ambition and you
  can't get your honor to rise. A man so young.

(*She shakes her head and sits at the piano. She beings to play
something [MacDowell, Andantino and Allegretto, but here it is
played because of time].*)

Scene 24

(TEDDY and ALICIA.)

TEDDY: Alicia, the hour is upon you. He's taking over your house. There is an American battleship in the harbor.

ALICIA: Don't tell me all these things! I only want my son!

TEDDY: Do you even have ransom money for Carlito? I'm glad to pay the ransom, that's no problem. But the fact is the house is decreasing in value by the moment.

ALICIA: They want *people* released. You can't throw your money around here, Teddy. It's *people* they want.

TEDDY: Money talks. Let me buy the house.

ALICIA: You are talking about the house? Even as my son is in danger?

TEDDY: At least if you give me ownership of the house, I can find other ways to control Antonio.

ALICIA: Everyone tells me I am not realistic. Now you be realistic. No one controls Antonio! No one! You want the house? It's yours! I ask one thing. One thing! *(She is hyperventilating.)*

(Pause.)

ALICIA: Do you know what it has been to take care of a piano in Cuba? To bring a piano to Cuba? With this weather? To care for it every day! To keep its keys just right? Do you know? Do you have any idea? This humidity?

TEDDY: Have faith!

ALICIA: Faith? Faith? Can't you think of anything better to say? "Have faith." I have my faith but the gods are in love with these two powers and their big balls. America. And Spain. America. And Spain. And what is Cuba? Eh? This little island. "Have faith." "Have—faith." I am Catholic. I am a daughter of Chango! *(She pulls out her strings of beads from inside her dress top.)* I have *two* faiths. I "have" "faith." While I have been worshiping the gods. Spain, and America have been molesting my Cuba. *And where is my son?* Cuba will never be the same. It will never be the same.

(She leaves.)

Scene 25

(Just before dawn.)

*(*MARTINE *is playing Schubert [same as before, "Ungeduld"].* ALICIA, *wearing a nightgown, is singing and dancing. There is a lit candle on the piano.* SUSANNA *enters. She blows out the candle.)*

SUSANNA: Señor the general has asked me to pack your things whether you assist or not.

*(*MARTINE *leaves, taking a cue from* SUSANNA.*)*

Have you heard drums in the night, Señora? I threw shells. I see it now. This trouble with Carlito has come from you.

ALICIA: What have I done?

SUSANNA: You did not obey Chango.

ALICIA: When?

SUSANNA: You saw the big storm in the fire. The big explosions.

ALICIA: I remember them.

SUSANNA: I have thrown the shells. Those big explosions are going to be in Havana. Very soon.

ALICIA: I only think of Carlito.

SUSANNA: Pay attention. Try! You must not stay in this house. There is something evil here.

ALICIA: Antonio is what is evil here.

SUSANNA: You are right. I have read his mind. He has no intention of bringing Carlito back.

ALICIA: You read his mind.

SUSANNA: He came to me in my bed!

ALICIA: You *let* him?

(*Long pause.*)

SUSANNA: I know. I know. But, Señora, I drew him to me. It was the only way to get close enough to read his mind, and there I saw it, Antonio refusing to meet the demand of the insurrectos. Saying, "I will not release the people, I will give you one boy for one boy." Over and over. He was remembering it as he had his way with me! It's in his mind! What he has done!

ALICIA: I only want Carlito!

SUSANNA: Señora. Have you looked outside? The Spanish flag is flying from the roof of the well. I tell you that the insurrectos will not bring back Carlito to a place which is flying the flag of Spain. Finally, you must obey Chango. To pray is one thing, to obey is another. Do you remember when you saw in the fire the house in the south of Spain with lace curtains flying in the wind? I understand it now, Chango was telling you to go there. Trust Chango, Señora. Have faith. I know that Chango will do something in Havana very soon. Very big, and this will light the sky, this will show us the way. You go first. In the fire first was the picture of you, then of Carlito.

ALICIA: I cannot leave without Carlito.

SUSANNA: You *must*. You have made Chango very angry by staying as long as you did. If you remember, Señora, we saw this one month before Señor Antonio came, and you did not believe Chango then. You stayed.

ALICIA: But you said when we saw in the fire the house in the south of Spain that it was a sign that Carlito's manhood was coming! That is what you said Susanna. You *must* remember! Why is Chango angry with me? You did the interpretation! Why isn't he angry with you?

(Pause.)

SUSANNA: At least do this, Señora, pack your things, and I will see what I can do to get Carlito set free for you.

ALICIA: You can do something?

SUSANNA: I can try. I only wish you had some money, Señora.

ALICIA: You know I do not have any money, Susanna.

(Pause. She abruptly gets up, goes to the piano, and takes money from a safe which is behind a false front above the keys.)

SUSANNA: Do you only have Spanish money? I need American money.

(ALICIA *looks again and then thrusts American money, taking back the Spanish money.*)

SUSANNA: No, no. I'll take both. I'll need both. In the meantime, pack your things and we will place them at the garden door, so that Chango can see that you are ready to make your peace with him.

(ALICIA *exits.* SUSANNA *follows.*)

Scene 26

(There are trunks and other luggage at the garden doors. ANTONIO *enters from the garden, stepping around the luggage.* ROSA *comes in with a suitcase and adds it to the collection.* SUSANNA *follows.)*

ANTONIO: How I love the look of luggage packed. Susanna! You are a master! A job well done. *(He surveys the luggage again, genuinely fascinated.)* But tell me, how did you do this?

SUSANNA: I lied, Señor. I do not like to lie. It is against my religion.

ANTONIO: You are voodoo. Voodoo does not believe in telling the truth!

SUSANNA: *(Taking a cigar from a humidor and lighting it.)* But, Señor, I am Catholic.

ANTONIO: Enh-henh. So tell me, what was this lie?

SUSANNA: I told her I brought you to my bed, and there I convinced you to bring Carlito back, through my powers, with my sex.

ANTONIO: *(Begins to guffaw.)* You! Are an alchemist. Alicia has known me since I was a boy in short pants. She knows that I do not like Africans. Even when my testicles were the size of a rooster's balls, I would have had the sense not to go near an African woman! I believe that you Africans are little more than apes.

(Pause.)

SUSANNA: At any rate, Señor, they will return any moment.

I would like to settle this debt now.

ANTONIO: Oh. Of course. (*Starts to take out his wallet.*)

SUSANNA: But, Señor. I don't want Spanish money.

ANTONIO: What?

SUSANNA: I don't want Spanish money.

ANTONIO: If it's American money you want, I certainly don't have any of that!

SUSANNA: Then I want land.

ANTONIO: Really, Susanna. "Desdemona" owns the land for now. Until Spain kicks the U.S. out of the Americas!

SUSANNA: But Señor, you and I both agree: That will never happen. I am happy to have land in Spain, or Venezuela, or the Philippines, or anywhere you suggest. Wherever you have land. You *do* have land in all those places don't you Señor General?

ANTONIO: You would have to travel there.

SUSANNA: I would like to travel.

ANTONIO: I won't get involved with land. I'll give you American money. That's all. What would you Africans do with land? You wouldn't know how to take care of it.

(Takes out his wallet.) I think this should cover it.

SUSANNA: I know how to count American money, Señor. *(Pause.)* Moreover I do not like to lie when I use my powers of persuasion. I did not expect that I would have to go that far, when we negotiated my fee, for "convincing." My fee was for "convincing." I did not know I would have to lie.

(ANTONIO takes out more money. SUSANNA stuffs it in her apron. She puts out her cigar and rises.)

And, Señor. Alicia is expecting that Carlito will be returned just before she leaves.

ANTONIO: Enh-henh.

SUSANNA: I promised her he would be here.

ANTONIO: She believed you! She is as mad as a monkey.

SUSANNA: She trusts me, Señor.

ANTONIO: Women! You have so much faith. That's why you got your balls chopped off when the apple fell on you!

(MONROE enters, carrying a piece of paper.)

MONROE: An American battleship has been blown up in the harbor outside Havana.

ANTONIO: What are you talking about? If there was a ship blown up, my men would have told me.

MONROE: Perhaps their wires are not as powerful as mine.

(ANTONIO *snatches it.*)

ANTONIO: An American battleship has been blown up in the harbor. *The Maine.* This is not possible.

MONROE: We are at war with you.

ANTONIO: We? We? I hear they hang the likes of *you* from trees. You monkey! If you were in the U.S. with "Desdemona," you would be swinging from a tree!

MONROE: America will declare war, against Spain.

ANTONIO: For what? Blowing up a ship? If Spain had anything to do with this I would know! Susanna! What do you know about the insurrectos blowing up an American ship?

SUSANNA: Why would the insurrectos blow up an American ship? They hate you. They hate Spain. They believe America will help them get Spain out of here forever.

ANTONIO: Is it possible that the Americans have blown up their own ship? Could they be that crazy?

(HENRY *enters.*)

ANTONIO: I told you to go home!

HENRY: Señor General, what do you know about this ship that blew up?

(ANTONIO *takes out his revolver and shoots at him.*)

HENRY: Just thought I'd ask.

Scene 27

(ALICIA *is at the piano, dressed for travel. She and* MARTINE *are playing Granados's "Oriental."* EDUARDO *enters through the garden doors with* TEDDY. *He is also dressed for travel.* ANTONIO *enters.*)

ANTONIO: Everything in order?

EDUARDO: We are ready.

ALICIA: And where is Carlito?

ANTONIO: I regret—you are going to have to leave without Carlito. The situation is impossible.

(ALICIA *sits back down at the piano. She starts to strike the keys.* ANTONIO *walks over and takes the red cloth. He puts it over her hands.*)

ALICIA: Eduardo? Are you going to let this general strike your wife? Or touch me? Because however far he plans to go, he will go. I am not going to leave without Carlito.

ANTONIO: I would never strike you, my dear Alicia. You are the mother of my nephew, the only male heir to Lopez y Vargas.

ALICIA: (*Screaming.*) Susanna!!!! Susanna!!!!

TEDDY: Alicia. This is not good for you. Please.

(SUSANNA *comes rushing in.*)

ALICIA: They will not tell me where Carlito is. They know. Susanna. They know! They won't tell me.

TEDDY: I only bought your house, to help you. You can't make me a part of this.

ALICIA: Where is Carlito?!

ANTONIO: All right. All right.

ALICIA: He was supposed to be here before I left!!!!

ANTONIO: Where do you think I have been all day and night? Making a deal!!!!

EDUARDO: And?

ANTONIO: Don't make me tell this, brother. It is too painful.

EDUARDO: Tell it.

ANTONIO: Perhaps I can tell you and you will tell Alicia.

EDUARDO: Tell us both.

ANTONIO: He was found. In a ditch. With flies all over his body. Bleeding. Dead. Castrated. His clothing strewn about the road! He tried to get away.

ALICIA: I don't believe you!!!! I know that the people would not hurt Carlito!!!

ANTONIO: But the people did not take him. There were American shoes in the ditch.

ALICIA: I don't believe you!!!! I don't believe you!!!! Tell them, Susanna! Tell them!! It's not true! Tell them what you saw in the fire!

ANTONIO: *(Quickly, yelling.)* Susanna knows! Don't you, Susanna? Don't you?

SUSANNA: It is true, Señora.

ALICIA: Take me to the body.

TEDDY: Alicia.

ALICIA: Take me to the body.

ANTONIO: The body has been sent to Spain. You will meet it. *(ALICIA begins to scream uncontrollably.)*

(ANTONIO and EDUARDO try to control ALICIA. She falls with her entire weight onto MARTINE and sobs. SUSANNA and TEDDY pull her off of him and take her out of the room.)

I am deeply sorry, brother. Deeply grieved. *(Pause.)* There are doctors in Vienna who are working with women like Alicia. People have been talking about them. In Spain you might not hear it. When I was in Paris they were talking about them. Perhaps you should take her. Besides, she could be close to her Brahms there. *(He puts his hand to EDUARDO's back in a warm, paternal manner and walks him toward the hallway.)*

Scene 28

(In the sitting area there is now a long table with maps and warfare planning sheets. There is a rack of pistols and rifles, and a flag of Spain. MARTINE *is putting ammunition into a gun.* HAN *is cleaning guns.* CHAN *is looking out the window.)*

*(*SUSANNA *enters through the house carrying a sack.* ROSA *follows.)*

*(*ROSA *leaves.)*

SUSANNA: Whoever heard of falling asleep in the middle of the day, and allowing a girl to come and steal the ammunition right off your chest? A child can steal a gun from these Spanish men. Rosa has stolen six guns.

CHAN: The girl has a dead eye. I have taken her to the hills to shoot moving things.

SUSANNA: I don't want you taking the girl to the hills to shoot moving things. That is not her job in the revolution. She will be a servant of Santa Barbara!

CHAN: You start this babbling about Santa Barbara! Where have you been? You're late.

HAN: Here comes the pig. *(Everyone jumps to attention.)*

*(*CHAN, MARTINE, *others disappear.* SUSANNA *remains.)*

ANTONIO: Tell your servants to get me something to drink! It's so damned hot out there! Where the hell are all my men? I just fought a battle which will get me a statue in the main plaza of Madrid and not a man in sight to greet me?

(There are several explosions, one right after the other. CHAN enters.)

CHAN: American troops! Approaching. Señor Antonio, you are flying the flag of Spain. They will take this house, and this is not a Spanish house, it is a Cuban house.

ANTONIO: It's a Spanish house as long as I am here!!!!! Finally!!!!!! America!! You have come to see me. Let's finish this once and for all! At least come finish with me!!! Ha!!!! You are walking in the lion's mouth!!

(HAN and MARTINE reenter with guns.)

ANTONIO: Are you working for the Americans now?

HAN: We are working for us.

ANTONIO: I'm not worth the blood on your floor. The Americans will come in here and turn the place into a brothel and a saloon.

(SUSANNA appears behind ANTONIO with a machete.)

SUSANNA: Señor General Antonio Lopez y Vargas! I am Susanna the servant of Chango and Santa Barbara! Don't yell, Señor. If you yell, you will turn into a woman.

(She raises the machete.)

(Lights out.)

(Bells ring wildly, as in a wedding.)

Scene 29

(HAN *is holding a Cuban flag.* MARTINE *and* CHAN *are also present.* MARTINE *plays a song of the Cuban Revolution.*)

(HENRY *enters. He is looking wildly around the room, looking at guns, maps, et cetera, and writing madly.*)

HAN: Lopez y Vargas is dead!

Where is it? The death of Spain in the Americas. Where's his body?

(CHAN *enters with the Spanish flag.*)

Where's the General's body?

CHAN: Why?

HENRY: I don't believe it til I see it.

(HENRY, *with his camera, follows the trail of blood.* MARTINE *plays the song of the Cuban revolution even louder.*)

Ah, this must be Antonio's blood, on the floor. My God! Look at this blood. What'd you do, decapitate him? (*He laughs, they stare.*)

Scene 30

(HENRY, CHAN, HAN, *and* MARTINE.)

(TEDDY *enters.*)

HENRY: Antonio's troops have packed up and gone. So, is this house yours now?

TEDDY: Are you still working on that story? Why don't you move on to the Philippines? This has reached its crest and the crest is falling. I'm starved. Chan, could you make us something for lunch? Anything?

CHAN: I don't work here anymore.

TEDDY: I was hoping you would stay. For now. I have to be here for another month or so.

CHAN: To complete all your sales?

TEDDY: You don't have to say it with such hatred. I thought we were friends.

(*Pause.*)

CHAN: I can see where this is going. Our revolution is for what? For you? To buy property here? Is that all? It's time for me to leave.

HENRY: How about staying just long enough to cook one lunch?

CHAN: Señora Theodora can cook your lunch. She owns the house, that means she owns the kitchen.

TEDDY: Chan, call me Teddy and take my advice.

CHAN: Señora Alicia took your advice, and look what happened to her.

TEDDY: It was for her own good.

CHAN: Why can't I decide for myself what's for my own good?

TEDDY: It's hopeless. This revolution. America is only here to protect its larger interests.

CHAN: I know all of that. I have read Martí.

TEDDY: And it is I who introduced you to Martí in the first place, Chan. I am the first one who sent you his writings.

HENRY: Chan, if you've read Martí, you would know that the real monster is America.

CHAN: You can't scare me.

HENRY: We're not trying to scare you. We just want you to cook us some lunch!

(He wanders off.)

TEDDY: I can be of use to you. Real use. I can supply you with ammunition. Machinery.

CHAN: Why would you do that?

TEDDY: I don't care about this war. It's a stupid war. I don't care about Spain, I care about these plantations. That's all. You want ammunition, machinery? You want Monroe to work with you? Your insurrectos could use some of his help. I'll let you have Monroe. He can help you communicate across distances. And if you want, you can come back to America with us. You can work for us—not a servant, a good job.

CHAN: The point is, I don't want your help.

(CARLITO *comes in, perfectly normal.* TEDDY *gasps.*)

CARLITO: Hello, Teddy.

TEDDY: Carlito!

(*Lights out.*)

Scene 31

(MARTINE *is at the window, armed.* CHAN *is going through* ANTO-NIO'*s maps and records.* HENRY'*S camera is downstage.* HAN *is looking at it.* TEDDY *is smoking.*)

TEDDY: You knew all along. You knew exactly where he was.

(MARTINE *turns to look at her, and sighs.*)

You all knew!!!!

MARTINE: It won't get us statues on the beach, but we did our part.

TEDDY: Arranging the kidnap of Carlito was your part? The very child who loved you all as if you were his parents.

MARTINE: His parents were children.

CHAN: We are his parents.

HAN: Susanna was the mother he never had. His mother was in love with the piano.

TEDDY: What are you doing?

HAN: Taking a photograph of you.

TEDDY: I don't want a photograph taken!!!

CHAN: You've created a pretty big problem for yourself Teddy.

You stole Alicia's house from under her nose, you made her vulnerable by aiding in the kidnap of her son. . . .

TEDDY: *You* kidnapped him!!!! *(Pause.)*

(The camera flashes, in its nineteenth-century way.)

(Pause.) Chan, I thought we were friends.

CHAN: You sent me the writings of Martí. For that I am grateful.

TEDDY: I think of you as a brother. I *love* you.

CHAN: Brother and sister we will never be.

HAN: Chan is nobility.

(HAN leaves HENRY'S camera, and takes a post at the window, with a gun.)

CHAN: I, am a descendent of Confucius. You, are the daughter of . . .

HENRY: *(Entering, carrying a large ripped painting.)* An American robber baron.

MARTINE: We told you to leave the premises.

HENRY: That's all well and good, but my boss has instructed me to stay until American troops arrive.

CHAN: Well, are they coming or not?

HENRY: They haven't won the war yet. They'll come if they win the war. You're not going to be any better off with the Americans. The Americans will not be coming to release you from the Spanish, they will be coming to protect American-owned property.

MARTINE: We really don't need you to tell us our history.

TEDDY: *(Truly horrified.)* What is that you're carrying?

HENRY: Oh. In case anybody's interested, all of the art is okay and still hanging safely, everything survived Antonio's drunken troops, except for this.

TEDDY: That is a Velázquez!!!!! What are the paintings doing here??? They were to have been packed up and sent to my home in New York months ago!!!!!

CHAN: We are not your servants madam.

TEDDY: The art was to be shipped to New York, and you and this entire staff would take care of this house until I got everything in order!!! That was part of the deal.

HAN: A deal with Eduardo, not with us.

TEDDY: Frankly Han, it's just not your place to say that to me.

MARTINE: I am afraid you cannot tell her what to say or not to say.

HENRY: Is it true what the American journalists say about you?

MARTINE: Are you talking to me?

HENRY: That you have been hanging around the American

troops giving sexual favors to the American soldiers in exchange for money?

MARTINE: Why do you ask? Would you like a favor or two?

HENRY: Only if you are cutting your prices.

TEDDY: (*Screaming.*) I WANT THIS ART PACKED UP IMMEDIATELY. AND I WANT LUNCH PREPARED IMMEDIATELY. I HAVE NOT EATEN IN TWO DAYS. DO YOU HEAR ME? IMMEDIATELY. COOK ME SOME LUNCH!

(*She grabs* HAN.)

HAN: We are in the midst of a war right now. It's hard to ship things. Besides, there are pirates, in the waters. Everything is in chaos madam. It's not a time to be worried about art. If people don't survive this, how can paintings? I myself am more concerned about the people.

CHAN: Like all of the people who died in the reconcentrados. Yes we kidnapped Carlito, but it would seem to me, that for all the letters you wrote to me for all those years about Cuban independence, you would understand why we thought that putting the life of Carlito in danger may have helped to relieve a few of the thousands of people who were being treated in the most inhumane way by the general. But no, your dear Alicia was so wrapped up in her own fantasies that she couldn't get her own husband to do something about it.

TEDDY: You get those paintings packed up and sent to New York, or I will get the entire United States army in here! Oh

I feel as though I am losing my mind. Really, am I going mad?

HENRY: You're not going mad.

TEDDY: You shut up!!! What do you know? What do you know???? About America?

HENRY: I think I know quite a lot.

CHAN: You have no idea madam, what life was like in those reconcentrados, and the fact is, we took very good care of Carlito. Very good care. But no one seemed to be able to humanize the pig, the general. No one, and they left. They actually left! Taking the word of a known liar that their son was dead. A known *liar*. If I remember correctly the general, as a boy was always in the habit of telling lies, I believe he once told Alicia that her favorite horse would be killed in order to get her to lower her panties. So, poor Carlito. I'd say his parents didn't care too much for him, if they couldn't come out of their fog long enough to realize that they were taking the word of a known liar, a known liar, someone who had lied to them since they were children.

TEDDY: *(Calmly.)* Is that what you told Carlito?

(SUSANNA *enters briskly, with* ROSA *who is carrying a bucket.* ROSA *drops to the floor and starts scrubbing.)*

Susanna. Please. Help me.

SUSANNA: Chan? Do you have a price yet?

TEDDY: That's all I want! Is a price, Susanna. I have been in here for an hour asking for a price. I will pay anything for Carlito. Alicia is in an asylum in Germany right now, from this awful awful situation. Going absolutely mad because she thinks her son is dead. She has no idea that the very people she has loved and helped for all these years kidnapped her own son! *(Pause.)* Were you a part of this Susanna? Were you?

SUSANNA: Chan? Why do you not yet have a price for Carlito?

CHAN: The boy is not for sale.

SUSANNA: Since when?

CHAN: The boy is not for sale. And this girl should no longer have to scrub floors.

SUSANNA: Look at his blood all over the floor. You are fighting with Señora Theodora because of the blood on the floor. Why else would you fight with someone who has done so much for you over the years? The girl must scrub the floor. She is a servant of Santa Barbara, and that is her job.

CHAN: Her job is to go into the hills and learn to shoot moving things. She has a dead eye, and that will be very useful in the revolution.

SUSANNA: The revolution, the revolution takes a long time. At this moment, she must scrub the floor, unless you would like to.

(CHAN drops to his knees, and pushes ROSA in the direction of MARTINE.)

CHAN: Show Madam Theodora what you have learned during the war. The girl is a servant of the revolution, she is not a servant of Santa Barbara.

(MARTINE *leaves his post, goes to the piano and beckons* ROSA. ROSA *follows* MARTINE *to the piano. He plays a few notes and* ROSA *begins to play Chopin waltz 34, number 2.*)

HENRY: Now, *that's* amazing.

HAN: What's so amazing about it? Europe has prodigies. Why shouldn't we Cubans have prodigies?

(SUSANNA *is smoking a cigar and counting piles of money.*)

SUSANNA: Chan is not a businessman. Chan is a warrior. But what Chan does not understand is that warriors are now businessmen. Those are the real warriors. The warriors are the men who sell coal and steel and ships and forests and newspapers, am I right Henry? The warriors are the men who create wars. Chan still thinks that a warrior carries a sword. Chan the real war is fought with dollars. What is your price Chan?

(MONROE *enters.*)

CHAN: The boy is not for sale, he will stay here and help build the Cuba of tomorrow.

MONROE: I have just gotten a wire that the Americans have declared victory.

SUSANNA: *(To Monroe.)* Victory? Over whom?

MONROE: Why, the Spanish. Of course.

SUSANNA: And we Cubans?

MONROE: The wire says nothing about Cubans.

HENRY: I gotta get out of here.

(MARTINE *blocks his exit.*)

First you asked me to leave. Now you want me to stay.

MARTINE: If the Americans are headed up here, you are going to be here when they come.

HENRY: I doubt if the Americans will come up here. Why would they come here? They defeated the Spanish here already. They have no reason to come.

MARTINE: Except to protect American property.

(MARTINE *shoves* HENRY *into a chair.*)

HENRY: If the Americans do come, I'm sure one of your customers would be happy to do business with you.

CHAN: (*Rising from the floor, with the scrub brush in his hand.*) The Americans better be ready to do business with all of us, after all we did to help them capture the general and this house!!!! About how much money should we expect from the Americans Susanna?

(CARLITO *enters, as* MONROE *leaves.*)

SUSANNA: Ah Carlito, my little man. Come to Susanna.

(*He does. She smooths his head as she used to. She kisses him.*)

My little man. You are looking so well. Susanna is so proud of you. Now you are good. And strong.

TEDDY: (*Crying.*) Oh Carlito, you are so thin.

CARLITO: I am only thin because I no longer eat sugared treats, which are for women, not for men.

SUSANNA: Carlito, what would you like to do? The Americans have declared victory over Spain. The war is over. We don't have to fight Spain, and we shouldn't fight America. You are free to do as you please.

CARLITO: Ah, but Susanna, one day we will have to fight America, because they are very big. And we are so small. And that which is big always tries to kill that which is small. It is a law of human nature. But there is great promise in that which is small, if we are clear.

(TEDDY *is sobbing uncontrollably.*)

Aunt Teddy, please don't cry. You know how it breaks my heart to see you or my mami when you cry.

HAN: Carlito, do you want to go to Spain to be with your mami and papi or do you want to stay in Cuba and become a great leader?

CARLITO: I have work to do. I will lead my people. I must stay.

My mami would be proud. She is the one who whispered to me every night at bedtime "Cuba Libre."

SUSANNA: You see Señora, you have to make a big price. He is very valuable.

TEDDY: (*She stops crying.*) What do you want?

SUSANNA: This house. This land. And you take the boy.

(MONROE *enters, escorting two American soldiers, one* WHITE OFFICER, *and one* BLACK ENLISTED MAN.)

WHITE AMERICAN OFFICER: We are here under authority of the United States army to protect this property and any American citizens in it.

(MARTINE *raises his rifle. The* BLACK AMERICAN SOLDIER *shoots his rifle out of his hand.*)

WHITE AMERICAN OFFICER: Which ones of you are American citizens?

HENRY: (*To the black man.*) You must be a buffalo soldier.

TEDDY: The boy comes with us.

WHITE AMERICAN OFFICER: Is he an American?

TEDDY: No, but he belongs to me.

BLACK SOLDIER: What about the girl?

TEDDY: She's one of theirs.

(The BLACK AMERICAN SOLDIER *watches* ROSA *as she begins to play MacDowell, from the beginning of the play.)*

HENRY: How'd you know we were here?

MONROE: I sent a wire.

WHITE AMERICAN OFFICER: No one is getting wires through, at least not in this area. Cuban rebels are burning property as soon as they find out it's owned by Americans. You have to get out of here.

BLACK AMERICAN SOLDIER: *(To no one in particular.)* How does she do that? Is that a real piano?

(Lights down as the BLACK AMERICAN SOLDIER *starts to take* SUSANNA *as a prisoner.)*

End of play

TALK TO ME
Travels in Media and Politics

Believing that character and language are inextricably bound, Anna Deavere Smith sets out to discern the essence of America by listening to its people and trying to capture its politics. She travels to locations that range from the presidential conventions of 1996 to a women's prison in Maryland. Memoir, social commentary, and meditation on language, *Talk to Me* is as ambitious as it is compellingly unique.

Biography/Autobiography/Political Science/0-385-72174-9

FIRES IN THE MIRROR
Crown Heights, Brooklyn, and Other Identities

In August 1991, simmering hostilities in the racially polarized neighborhood of Crown Heights, Brooklyn, exploded after an African American boy was killed by a car in a rabbi's motorcade and a Jewish student was slain in retaliation. Derived from interviews with a wide range of people who experienced or observed the Crown Heights riots, *Fires in the Mirror* is Anna Deavere Smith's extraordinary portrayal of the events and emotions leading up to and following the incident.

Current Affairs/Performing Arts/0-385-47014-2

TWILIGHT: LOS ANGELES, 1992
On the Road: A Search for American Character

Twilight: Los Angeles, 1992 is Anna Deavere Smith's stunning work of "documentary theater" in which she uses the exact words of people who experienced the Los Angeles riots to expose and explore the devastating human impact of that event. With brilliant emotional accuracy, this work is distinguished both as a commentary on racial conflict as well as a stunning dramatic masterpiece.

Current Affairs/Performing Arts/0-385-47376-1